How to Profit from Your Faults

Joseph Tissot

HOW TO PROFIT *from* YOUR FAULTS

BASED ON THE WRITINGS OF
ST. FRANCIS DE SALES

Scepter

Originally published in 1878 as *L'Art d'utiliser ses fautes.*
The English translation was published in 1996 by Scepter, London.
This edition published with the permission of Scepter, London.

Published by Scepter Publishers, Inc., New York
(800) 322–8773 / www.scepterpublishers.org

ISBN 1-59417-013-4
ISBN 978-1-59417-013-3

Text composition in Monotype Apollo fonts

Fourth Printing, August 2009
Printed in the United States of America

Contents

Foreword 7

Part I

1 Our failings do not surprise us 11
2 Our faults do not upset us 20
3 Never be discouraged by our faults 32

Part II

4 Humility through self-knowledge 47
5 Getting to love our misery 62
6 Confidence in God's mercy (i) 75
7 Confidence in God's mercy (ii) 86
8 Strengthening our perseverance 94
9 How to become more fervent 104
10 The practice of making satisfaction 111
11 Devotion to our Lady 121

Notes 135

Foreword

to the Sixth French edition

It gives me great satisfaction to see the publication of the sixth edition of *L'Art d'utiliser ses fautes*. This will allow the book to be more widely available, and it will be able to do good—which, thanks be to God, is already happening—to a large number of souls.

The pieces of accompanying advice which the Doctor of piety offers are not meant only for those who want to be pious. They are directed also at sinners who are moved when they hear St. Francis de Sales referring to the lengths to which divine mercy goes to make conversion easier. It is a love filled with compassion, which follows up the prodigal; the fatherly welcome that awaits them on their return; the favors that reward their repentance. Even the hardest of hearts soften with the hope of occupying a place in the home of the Father of the family.

Someone has said that whoever reads a few lines of this work after committing a fault will find through them, and with the Lord's help, the grace to get up again. *How to Profit from Your Faults* enables one to detest those faults and to avoid them. Admiration for the divine goodness, which so generously forgives and which so liberally restores, makes one feel a love for such a good God having being born; one experiences a more loving sorrow for having saddened him, and one understands better those words which, in my judgment, are the best praise for this book: "It inspires one to resolve not to sin again."

I have not wanted to shorten the text in this edition. Indeed, I have added some quotations; and, to help the reader, I have divided the book into sections and chapters.

Now it is left for me only to repeat the petition I made to the Sacred Heart of Jesus when I consecrated this book to him for the first time sixteen years ago. May the adorable Heart deign to bless it and use it for his glory, making it produce fruits of conversion in sinners and perseverance and perfection in the just.

Joseph Tissot

Missionary of St. Francis de Sales
Annecy, France
First Friday of April 1894

Part I

I

Our Failings Do Not Surprise Us

Imperfections and defects are always with us

It is both the glory and the torment of fallen man that he cannot get used to having come down in the world. As with a prince reduced to being a commoner, his descent from royal parentage confers on him no advantage whatsoever. But in his heart of hearts he cherishes the memory of his high-born origin and of a lost innocence that ought to have been his noble inheritance. He can scarcely smother an exclamation of amazement at the repeated evidence of his downfall, like one who has incurred some unmerited misfortune.

He is like a Samson who, drained of his power by the wicked hand that has shorn him of his hair, staggers to his feet as the Philistines shout, "Get up!" He is confident as he rises that, as on previous occasions, he will be more than a match for his foes, only to discover that the strength he could call on in the past has now failed him (see Judges 16: 20).

To whatever extent such aristocratic sentiment be present in us, its consequences are unfortunate and have to be combatted. As shall become evident, discouragement means spiritual diminution and loss for the soul. But it cannot overcome us if surprise, which seems inevitably attendant upon a failure, is not allowed to open up a path for it. St. Francis de Sales forewarns us against precisely this danger.

Together with other eminent doctors and perspicacious minds, the saintly bishop was often moved to pity at the spectacle of man's feebleness. "Human misery, human misery . . . ," he would repeat, "how we are set about by weakness! What else can be looked for in us but falls?" His words and his writings all show that, from the heights of sanctity he had reached, he perceived with special clarity, and sounded with his penetrating gaze, the abyss of wretchedness and misery that original sin has struck deeply into our being. His open spirit was constantly aware of it in his dealings with souls who turned to him for spiritual direction, and he never wearied of reminding them of their fragile condition. "You live, according to what you tell me," he wrote to a lady, "with a thousand imperfections. It is true, my sister; but do you not try incessantly to make them die? What is certain is that as long as we live weighed down and oppressed by such a corruptible body as we have, there will always be *something* in us that falters. . . ."

Elsewhere he writes: "You complain that many imperfections and defects intermingle in your life, running counter to your desire for the perfection of purity in your love for God. I reply that it is not possible for us to become completely disengaged from self until God carries us to heaven. We shall not carry a treasure of the greatest possible value while we are burdened down with the weight of our own selves. . . . Isn't it generally true that no saint could become so holy had he not always been subject to imperfections?" [1]

Self-love remains with us

Faith teaches us, in effect, that evil inclinations remain in us, at least in germinal form, until death. And, in the absence of a special privilege—as in the case of our Lady, which the Church recognizes—nobody can avoid all venial sins, or at least the non-deliberate ones. In practice, we lose sight of this hard truth, and it would be salutary to review the way our Saint develops it, using simple language. "Let us not imagine that while we are in this life we can live without imperfection. For this is simply not possible, whether we be superior or inferior, since all of us are human. And this is a truth of which we all have to be convinced in order not to be astonished to see ourselves subject to such imperfections. Our Lord commanded us to say every day in the Our Father: *'forgive us our trespasses as we forgive those who trespass against us'*. The command admits of no exceptions. All of us need to make this same daily petition." [2]

"Self-love can be changed in ourselves, but it never dies. From time to time, and on various occasions, it seems to throw out new shoots. Its renewed sprouting shows that even if it has been cut back right to the ground it has not been eradicated. At times it seems inert; but we should not find it strange that it is still alive. Just as the motionless fox appears to be asleep and then suddenly leaps upon its prey, we too must be constantly vigilant and be prepared to defend ourselves against the attacks of self-love with care and patience. And if it does happen sometimes to wound us, the injury will heal if we retract what it made us say, or undo what it made us do." [3]

But our cure can be no more than temporary, and will last only until some fresh recurrence of the malady assails us. "Until we are in Paradise," [4] adds our Saint, and as long as this life lasts, and no matter how great be our good will, "it will be necessary to be patient, for what we have is a human and not an angelic nature." [5] We ought therefore to resign ourselves to living, in the words of a celebrated ascetic, as "incurable spirits" in this world.

Knowledge of self is vital

It is principally for the benefit of souls who are beginning to take the first steps on the road to perfection that St. Francis de Sales points out the necessity for practical knowledge of their weaknesses. They are those who, through inexperience, are more easily disconcerted when they have made a mistake, with apparently disastrous consequences. "To become perturbed and dismayed when one falls into sin is not to know oneself."

With what sensitivity our blessed Doctor reproves and instructs these souls! "You 'still' have, you tell me, this very acute sense of suffering injuries. But, my daughter, what does this 'still' refer to? Have you already vanquished many enemies of this kind?" [6]

"It is not possible for you to become mistress of your soul so soon, as if you were already completely in control of it. Be content with gaining, little by little, some small advantage over your dominant defect." [7]

"Our imperfections will accompany us to the grave. We cannot walk without touching the ground. It is not necessary for us to be down in the mud, but then neither is it necessary for us to think of flying, because we are fledglings and don't yet have wings." [8]

"The 'arrows' that fly to the heights (Ps 90:6) are the vain hopes and presumptions which, at the beginning of their conversion, certain souls desirous of perfection have of arriving quickly at their goal. They feel that in no time at all they are going to achieve the sanctity of a Teresa of Avila or a Catherine of Siena or of Genoa. Fine. This is all very well, but tell me this: 'Just how long a time are you thinking of spending in order to get there?—Three months; less if possible.—You do well to say 'if possible' for otherwise you can be out in your calculations. . . ." [9]

"St. Paul was purified in an instant; so were St. Catherine of Genoa, the Magdalen, and some other saints. But this sort of purification is completely miraculous. And it is just as extraordinary in the order of grace as the resurrection of bodies is in the order of nature. Therefore we ought not to seek it. 'Ordinary' purification and cure of souls, as of bodies, is won little by little as we progressively move from one arduous grade to the next, through the effort of work and with the passage of time. The angels on Jacob's ladder had wings but did not fly. They ascended and descended rung by rung. In the same way, the climb from sin to piety can be likened to the dawning of the day, in which the rising sun does not instantaneously put the darkness to flight, but dissipates it little by little. The cure that takes place gradually is more certain, for illnesses, both of the soul and the body, although they come at a gallop, go away on foot, step by step." [10]

"One has, then, to be patient, and not try to banish in one short day the many evil habits we have acquired in our life as a result of the lack of care we have taken of our spiritual health." [11]

The good Saint's conclusion has the same incessant counsel: "Although through our weakness we shall experience many falls, we ought not to be troubled in any way." [12]

Front-line soldiers also get wounded

No matter how advanced a soul may be on the way to perfection, no one has the right to be surprised at his own stumbling. Even to the most fervent religious St. Francis gave this same advice: "Is it such a great marvel to discover that we slip up sometimes?" [13]

"The feast of the Purification does not have an octave. Two resolutions we require to make: one, that we shall be aware of noxious plants in our garden; the other, that we shall resolutely determine to keep these unwelcome growths down, and weed them out ourselves, because our love of self will never die as long as this life lasts, and it will go on being the cause of such inopportune faults."[14]

"I see the tears of our poor sister X, and I reflect that all our childishness proceeds from none other than this root cause: that we forget the maxim of the saints, who advise us that we should begin each day the journey of our perfection. If we were to consider this, we would not find it at all strange to come across such misery in ourselves."[15]

"You may ask me what you ought to do in order to strengthen your bond with God in such a way that nothing can loosen it or sever you from him. Two things are needed for this—to die, and to be saved. After that there will be no more separation, and your spirit will be indissolubly bound and united to God."[16]

What could be more consoling than this advice for souls seriously disposed to give thanks to God for everything and dedicated to serving him in an intimate relationship? Such souls are convinced that they have even less excuse than others for the infidelities they are capable of, and it seems to them as though their falls from grace are in their case the more unaccountable. But this is far from being the opinion of teachers of the spiritual life. Father Grou says: "Ordinarily our lapses proceed from the impetuosity of the journey and the ardor that propels us, militating against a more cautious venturing forward. Timid and circumspect souls, ever peering to see where they must place the next secure footprint, forever apprehensive of taking a false step, fearful of getting splashed, necessarily do not advance as rapidly as the others—death always surprises them halfway across the road. The more saintly are not those who commit fewer faults, but those with higher courage, a larger generosity, and a greater love. They are those who make more demands on themselves and are not in constant dread of taking a tumble, being concerned more with advancing than with the possibility of falling and perhaps getting a little wet." [17]

St. John Chrysostom is of the same mind, and says the same in other words: "When a soldier in battle is wounded and gives ground a little, no one is so unreasonable or so ill-versed in military matters as to believe that such behavior is criminal. Only those are invulnerable who are far behind the lines and do not fight. Those who launch themselves forward bravely in assault against the enemy are the ones who take a hammering." [18]

Mortal sins should not surprise us

Could we also apply these reflections to mortal sin? Can it be recommended to seriously culpable souls that not even they should be thunderstruck at a fall that deprives them of God's friendship? St. Francis de Sales tends to use with them the same kind of words he has employed so far with more generous hearts.

Listen: "Dear Theotimus," he writes, "Heaven is shaken. Its gates tremble with horror, and the angels of peace are bewildered at the prodigious misery of the human heart when it casts aside such a splendid treasure in favor of such pitiful things. But think—have you ever noticed a small marvel, so commonplace as to be inconsiderable: when one pierces a well-filled cask the wine does not gush out unless there is air above it. This does not happen with barrels that are half-empty, for when they are perforated where the wine is, the liquor spouts out and spills. And this is similar to what happens in our earthly life;

although our souls may have in them an abundance of celestial love, they are never so full that in time of trial they cannot be subject to some loss of their precious contents. But there above, in Heaven, when the gentle beauty of God fills our entire understanding, when the unspeakable delight of his goodness satiates our whole will in such a way that the fullness of his love fills everything completely, there will be no object capable of penetrating our heart, or of drawing out of it a single spilt drop of the precious liquor of celestial love. And as for the possibility, as with our cask, that air can enter or be present and exert pressure from above—that is to say, that any temptation can cheat or surprise the intellect—this is not now possible, for it will be fixed forever in the apprehension of sovereign truth."[19]

Now we have heard it: a fall into sin, even into grave sin, should be no matter for astonishment as it would be in Heaven, where such falls are *impossible*. Here, below, there is no call for surprise, just as there is none when we see wine escape from a cask that has been broached.

Understanding

We say this in passing: what understanding we should have of our brothers and sisters if we were to meditate well on their counsels! We would be identifying ourselves with the ineffable patience of him who, before investing his Apostles with the power to forgive sins, recommended that they forgive, not seven times, but seventy times seven.

There is no doubt that such an understanding, applied to our own faults, as well as to our neighbors', should not lead to looking upon them with indifference. For it is one thing not to be surprised by them, and quite distinctly another not to detest faults themselves and make reparation for them. The sower is not surprised to see the weeds invade his field, but he does not stop pulling them out. Having said, without excepting mortal sin: "when you commit some fault do not be astounded";[20] having flatly stated: "If we knew well what we were, instead of being surprised at seeing ourselves fallen, we would be surprised how we could even stand";[21] St. Francis de Sales recommends that we do not remain down and muddy when we have taken a fall, adding immediately that "if the violence of a tempest were to make us queasy and induce in us a little sea-sickness, we would not find it strange, but, as soon as we could, we would get our breath back and pull ourselves together with renewed energy."[22]

"When your heart sinks, raise it gently, humbling yourself quietly in God's presence with the knowledge of your misery, without surprise at your fall, for it is no cause for marveling that sickness may make us ill, that weakness tends to diminish our strength, and that misery will cause us to be wretched. But hate with all your heart the offense you have committed against God, and, filled with courage and confidence in his mercy, get back on board to resume the voyage to Virtue, which you had abandoned."[23]

This text clearly leads us to understand that fruitful disposition ought to take the place of amazement at our faults: it is no less than the knowledge of our lowliness, and it is the first step on the road to humility. We shall speak of this in the second part of the book: for the moment, having made it plain that the sight of our falls ought not to produce astonishment, we shall show that there is even less reason for it to disconcert us.

2

Our Faults Do Not Upset Us

Effects of Sorrow

"*For godly grief produces a repentance that leads to salvation and brings no rgret, but worldly grief produces death,* says St. Paul (2 Cor 7: 10). Sorrow, then, can be either good or evil depending on how it affects us. True enough, it produces more bad effects than good; for it has only two good effects, namely, compassion and repentance. But it has six evil effects, namely, anxiety, sloth, wrath, jealously, envy, and impatience. This has caused Wisdom to say that *sorrow has brought death to many, and there is no profit in it* (Sir 30: 25). For two good streams flowing from sorrow as their source, there are six that are very evil." [24]

So the devil is prepared to go to great lengths to produce this *bad* sadness in us; and to discourage the soul and make it lose hope he tries above all to upset it. Here he does not need to make a great effort to produce motives. Is it not sufficient to have offended the Sovereign Majesty, to have insulted his infinite beauty, to have hurt the heart of the most lovable of fathers? Certainly, says St. Francis de Sales, one needs to have sorrow—but with true repentance and no ill-humored sadness mingled with despair and indignation. True repentance, like everything inspired by the good Spirit, is calm, *non in commotione*

Dominus[25]—the Lord was not in the earthquake. Where disquiet and distress begin, true sorrow gives way to the bad.

"Evil sorrow disturbs and upsets the soul, arouses inordinate fears, creates disgust for prayer, stupefies and oppresses the brain, deprives the mind of prudence, resolution, judgment, and courage, and destroys its strength. In a word, it is like a severe winter, which spoils all the beauty of the country and weakens all the animals. It takes away all sweetness from the soul and renders it disabled and impotent in all its faculties." [26]

Many souls will recognize in these symptoms the bewilderment they have been left with after their falls, and the havoc wreaked in them. They had begun with fervor; they had resolutely embarked on the journey, following the footsteps of the Master, scaling the steep slopes of Calvary. A fall overtook them, and they became bewildered. Nonetheless, they managed to pull themselves together: repentance and sacramental absolution repaired everything. But in spite of this, they did not stop looking anxiously at themselves again and again. They came to reexamine their barely healed wounds, getting stirred up and irritated, wishing impatiently to have them cured out of spite. They do not realize that "nothing better keeps stains in us than the pressure and the anxiety to get rid of them." [27]

Meanwhile, the pace is slackened. No longer do they run. They walk, and only with difficulty. They are slowed down. They are discontented with themselves, and almost even with God himself. They begin to lack confidence in prayer, and receive the sacraments with little disposition. All this continues until some special event, like a well-made confession or a retreat, allows the fervor they had at the beginning to return to these souls. But a little after this conversion, if they continue to be dominated by this bewilderment, new failures, or simply the memory of past falls, aggravate their discouragement. They return to the fray tired, and God does not want them to end up with an inertia with no remedy, a consequence of hesitation and slowness.

The slow pace of progress

What is it that has come to restrict your efforts? *You were running well: who hindered you from obeying the truth?*[28] asks the Apostle. Bewilderment, replies the author of *Philothea*: "If you had not been disconcerted at the first stumble, you would not have tripped." And so the lovable Saint insists on communicating to others "the sought-for peace, the most beloved, faithful, and perpetual guest of their heart."[29] Thus he recommends both calm and patience, *in the first place, with oneself*. "We must not be disturbed by our imperfections."[30] "Be warned against impulses and disquiet, for there is nothing that disturbs us more on the journey to perfection."[31]

"Why do birds and animals remain entrapped in their nets? Because when they have entered them, they get nervous, they flounder about in an unorganized way. And this makes them increasingly entangled. . . . If we fall into the net of our imperfections, we will not escape from them if we get flustered. We will, on the contrary, entangle ourselves even more."[32]

"The slow pace of our perfection has to be borne with patience, provided that on our part we always do whatever we can to continue advancing."[33]

We patiently hope, then, that we are going to improve, and, instead of becoming troubled by having done little in the past, we will try diligently to do more in the future."[34]

"We do not lose our peace when we see ourselves as beginners in the exercise of the virtues. For in such ventures all of us should always consider ourselves novices. We will be subject to trials all our lives. To feel that these difficulties have all been overcome is not only the surest sign that they have not been mastered but is also an indication of a lack of ability to continue under trial. The obligation to serve God and to progress in his love lasts until death.

"Someone may say to me: How can I avoid being saddened or upset if I realize that through my own fault I am being held back in the development of the virtues? I said in the *Introduction to the Devout Life*, and am delighted to repeat because it can never be said too often: 'It is a good thing to repent with a repentance both strong and calm, both constant and serene; but not one that upsets us, causes disquiet, or discourages us.' "[35]

Being patient, not anxious

We have seen—and it will become clearer with the texts we will quote shortly—that the holy Doctor not only recommends that just and innocent souls be calm and patient with themselves; they should take the same special approach with those unfortunate enough to have committed faults.

"If you sometimes feel impatient, do not be perturbed by this: try to recover rapidly and gently."[36]

"Do not be over-concerned by the outbursts of your self-love, which, doubtless, are frequent. They will never become dangerous if, without getting annoyed with yourself because they are a nuisance, without becoming perplexed because they are so many, you serenely say 'No!' Move on, with simplicity. Do not be so anxious for peace of spirit—then you will acquire it."[37]

"Be patient with the whole world, but, above all, with yourself. I want to tell you not to lose your serenity because of your imperfections, and always to have the zest to raise yourself up. It gives me joy to see that each day you begin again. There is no better way to finish life well than to return to the starting point always, and not ever to think that we have done enough." [38]

"However much we mortify the flesh, we will always find that it rebels. Distractions will always interrupt our concentration, and so forth, in everything. Are we going to get upset, to lose our peace, to be afflicted by this? In no way!" [39]

"Do not get annoyed or irritated when you find that all the imperfections you have spoken about to me begin to bubble up in your soul. No, I beg you. If, on the one hand, you certainly have to try to uproot them from the soul and to detest them in order to improve, it is, on the other hand, not necessary to inflict anguish on oneself, but rather to accept a punishment that encourages, that calms, and that gives rise to a serene and firm resolve to correct oneself." [40]

"One has to flee from evil, but without losing either serenity or peace. In any other way, when trying to avoid it, we ourselves stumble and give the enemy an opportunity to kill us off. Even penance itself should be carried out with peace. *It was for my welfare that I had great bitterness, but you have held back my life from the pit of destruction* (Is 38: 17)." [41]

"Nothing, but sin, should irritate or annoy. Even in the depths of this misfortune, there ought to be joyous and saintly consolation." [42]

"One who belongs to God never, ever, becomes sad, unless he has offended him. But this sorrow for the offense is founded on a deep, serene, and peaceful humility and submission. After this, one gets up again with a new tranquillity and perfect confidence in divine goodness, without chagrin or despair."[43]

"In summary: do not get angry, or at least, do not get irritated because you have been knocked off your stride. Do not lose your peace because these disturbing passions have upset you. Take hold of your heart and gently place it in the hands of our Lord."[44] "Although you feel filled with misery, encourage your heart to return to being at peace with yourself."[45]

"When you find your heart embittered, don't do any more than to grasp it by the fingertips, not by the hand, not brusquely. Patience with oneself is needed, and the heart must be happy. When it is agitated, one has to contain it as one controls a horse with a bridle, holding it firmly in place, and not allowing it to run riot with disordered sentiments."[46]

"Take a lot of care not to get agitated when you have committed some fault; but humiliate yourself as soon as possible, before God, with calm and loving sentiments. This will give birth to the confidence of resorting immediately to his goodness, and will inspire in you that certainty which enables one to make amends. . . . When it happens that you commit some fault, whatever it be, ask our Lord with simplicity for forgiveness, and tell him that you are sure that he loves you dearly and that he is going to pardon you."[47]

True and false humility—their fruits

To combat more effectively the restlessness that is so prejudicial, St. Francis de Sales tries to discover what is the ordinary cause, perhaps the only cause, of this lack of peace. It is self-love—the seeking of oneself. St. Teresa had already recognized this: "With true humility, when the soul recognizes evil, it becomes sad with a sorrow not accompanied by disquiet and agitation. It produces neither darkness nor dryness in spirit, but rather the opposite—consolation. The soul is afflicted because it had offended God; but on the other hand, it expands in the hope of his mercy. It has the light to feel ashamed, and to praise God, who has suffered so much. Furthermore, in false humility, which is given by the devil, there is no light for any good thing. It seems as though God has put fire and sword to everything. This is one of the more pernicious, subtle, and cunning inventions of the devil, as I have learned."[48]

So, to be perturbed after a sin is a very usual evil. "To be humiliated by one's own miseries," a holy priest has said, "is a good thing, and a few people understand it. To become agitated and to lose patience is something the whole world does, because self-love plays a major part in this kind of disquiet."[49]

Frederick Ozanam adds: "There are two classes of pride: the one that is satisfied with itself—this is the more usual and less dangerous. The other is discontented with itself, because it expects a lot of itself and feels cheated in its hope. This second kind of pride is more subtle and more dangerous."

Our good Saint tracks this self-love in all its disguises, masked with the blush of humility. The hurried steps that the soul wishes to take, not so much to cure itself but rather to feel convinced that it has been cured; the hidden deceptions that do not allow one to make peace with one's conscience, because it is more comfortable to consider it incorrigible; the melancholy that invades us; the incessant and exclusive reflection on our own faults and on ourselves; the need to lament in front of other men rather than before God, with a sneaky desire for consolation and commiseration from them: all this, the holy Doctor makes plain, "is produced by a particular spiritual father called *self-love*." [50]

"One of the better exercises in meekness we can perform is when the subject is in ourselves. We must not fret over our own imperfections. Although reason requires that we must be displeased and sorry whenever we commit a fault, we must refrain from bitter, gloomy, spiteful, and emotional displeasure. Many people are greatly at fault in this way. When overcome by anger, they become angry at being angry, disturbed at being disturbed, and vexed at being vexed. By such means they keep their hearts steeped in passion. It may seem that the second fit of anger does away with the first, but actually it serves to open the way for fresh anger on the first occasion that arises. Moreover, these fits of anger, vexation, and bitterness against ourselves tend to pride; and they spring from no other source than self-love, which is disturbed and upset at seeing that it is imperfect." [51]

"We ought not to feel confused with disquiet and sadness. This kind of confusion has its origin in self-love, because we are disgusted for not being more perfect, not so much out of love for God but because we love ourselves." [52] We find "such pleasure when we weep for our faults that we flatter our own self-love." [53]

"The excessive care we take over ourselves makes our spirit lose serenity, and leads to an extravagant and unbalanced humor. It happens when we meet with some contradiction, when we realize our lack of mortification, when we fall into one of our defects (however small it may be): it seems then that everything has gone under." [54]

"Self-love is one of the two sources of this turbulence. The other is that we have too high an estimation of ourselves. If we commit some sin or some imperfection, we find that we are astounded, disconcerted, impatient. And this result comes because we had considered ourselves to be something good and solid. Now, on seeing that we are nothing, on seeing ourselves down on the floor, we are enraged with disgust, deceived by our own strengths." [55]

"Take a lot of care not to lose your peace when you commit a fault. Nor should you be carried away by self-comparison; for all this comes from pride." [56]

Gentle treatment for the heart

This is the line of conduct St. Francis de Sales proposes against the agitation and sterile solicitude that self-love engenders. Such is the compassion the human heart inspires in him that it seems as if he takes its side when it weakens; and instead of flattening it and disturbing it even more, he tells us: "Do not torment your heart, even though it has, in some way, deviated. Take hold of it and return it gently to the straight and narrow." [57]

"Most beloved daughter: when we commit some fault, we should immediately examine our heart and ask it if it still has a living and whole desire to serve God. It will certainly reply, 'Yes.' And it would rather die a thousand deaths than give up this resolution. Ask it another question: Why then have you tripped up? Why are you cowardly? 'I have been caught off-guard, and I don't know how; but now it hurts me.' My daughter: One has to forgive it. It has not been unfaithful but weak. It needs gentle correction, not a broadside, so as not to irritate or upset it any more." [58]

"From the early morning, prepare your soul for calm; in the course of the day, try to recall this calm frequently. If you have some frustration, do not react; but without losing sight of it, humiliate yourself serenely before God and try to recover the serenity of your spirit. Tell your soul: 'Forward! We have taken a wrong step. Let us go ahead slowly and carefully.' And every time you fall, do the same."[59]

"We must be sorry for our faults, but in a calm, settled, firm way. When a judge is guided in his decisions by reason and proceeds calmly, he punishes criminals much more justly than when he acts in violence and passion. If he passes judgment hastily and passionately, he does not punish the crimes for what they really are, but for what they seem to him. So also we correct ourselves much better by calm, steady repentance than by that which is harsh, turbulent, and passionate. Violent repentance does not proceed according to the character of our faults but according to our inclinations. . . .

"Believe me, Philothea, a father's gentle, loving rebuke has far greater power to correct a child than rage and passion. So too when we have committed some fault, if we rebuke our heart with a calm, mild remonstrance, with more compassion for it than passion against it, and if we encourage it to make amends, then repentance conceived in this way will sink far deeper and penetrate more effectively than fretful, angry, stormy repentance.

"For my own part, if I had made a firm resolution not to yield to the sin of vanity, for example, and yet had seriously fallen into it, I would not reprove my heart in this manner: 'Aren't you wretched and abominable, you have made so many resolutions and yet let yourself be carried away by vanity? You should die for shame. Never again lift up your eyes to Heaven, blind, insolent traitor that you are, a rebel against your God!' I would correct it in a reasonable, compassionate way: 'Alas, my poor heart, here we are, fallen into the pit we were so firmly resolved to avoid! Well, we must get up again and leave it forever. We must call on God's mercy, and hope that it will help us to be steadier in the days to come. Let us start out again on the way of humility. Let us be of good heart and from this day be more on guard. God will help us. We will do better.' On the basis of such correction I would build a firm, solid resolution never again to fall into that fault, using the proper means of avoiding it under the advice of my director.

"However, if anyone finds that his heart is not sufficiently moved by this mild manner of correction, he may use a sharp, severe reproach and rebuke so as to excite it to a deeper sorrow. This must be on condition that after he has curbed and chided his heart in this rough way, he encloses all his grief and anger with sweet, consoling confidence in God, in imitation of that illustrious penitent who saw his afflicted soul and raised it up in this way: 'Why are you cast down, O my soul, and why are you disquieted within me? Hope in God, for I shall again praise him, my help and my God' (Ps 42: 5, 6)."[60]

Venial and mortal sin

It is not necessary to add that in all this advice, so full of love, there should be no word that allows the soul to fall asleep in sin. No one could be well advised to go to bed with a snake around his neck. Moreover, if one is in a state of mortal sin, faced with the idea of death and eternal punishment, how can one not but shudder? How can one not shake off an enemy who, with his arm, can at any instant drag us down to the abyss of eternal disgrace? And even if we are dealing with only venial sins, we cannot keep the soul with this dirt, which is so unpleasant to God, and whose weight leads us little by little, inexorably, toward mortal sin.

It is precisely so that we might be able to distance ourselves a little farther from sin that the holy Doctor forbids us from losing our peace. He well knows that nothing can be done in anger or when one is agitated. The good surgeon who has to carry out an amputation is kind to his patient and does not treat him brusquely; the operation will be more successful and be completed sooner if the patient is calm. Consequently, the most important thing is to restore calm and tranquillity.

What he advised others he practiced himself with his own imperfections. A man whom the Saint advised gives this example: "One day when I was fortunate enough to speak to him on spiritual matters, I told him that venial sins, even if they were small, caused a certain disquiet and perturbation in the heart. I had hardly finished speaking when he replied: 'Forgive me, but although we should detest venial sins, they ought not to perturb us. For disquiet is caused by self-love which is irritated because of the work it has to do to practice the virtues and because each day we have to begin again. On the other hand, dissatisfaction is an effect of grace, which inspires an aversion to everything that displeases our Creator.'

"This was his way of explaining the sorrow and regret we should have for our daily offenses. That is what he put into practice on similar occasions, asking our Redeemer for grace, but without getting bitter or irritated in the least. According to the Greeks, when Antheus fought Hercules, whenever he fell to the ground he immediately got up again, with renewed vigor and determination. In the same way, this magnanimous man fought with his passions. If he happened to take a false step, he got up with renewed courage and continued his job with patience and tranquillity, without getting irritated or disgusted with himself." [61]

3

Never Be Discouraged by Our Faults

We should not be discouraged on seeing our faults

A pious priest once made a retreat under the guidance of Father Roothran. During the few days it lasted, Father Roothran was called urgently to Rome, where he was to be elected general of the Society of Jesus. When he had wished everyone good-bye and was about to leave, he turned back and entered the room where the retreatant was. "Father," he said, "I have forgotten to give you a very important piece of advice: *Come what may, do not ever get discouraged.*"

Golden words. A recommendation that should be repeated to many souls. St. John Chrysostom never tired of repeating: "Do not ever despair! I will say this every time I address you, in all my conversations. And if you take heed, you will be healthy. Our salvation has two mortal enemies: presumption while innocent, and despair after a fall. The second is the more terrible." [62]

Truly, *in this hope we were saved* (Rom 8:24). "This virtue is like a strong chain that comes down from heaven and binds our souls. If these remain firmly bound, it gradually draws them up to sublime heights, and shields them from the torments of this life. But the soul overcome by discouragement is loosed from this holy anchor; it falls immediately and perishes into the abyss of evil.

"Our perfidious adversary does not ignore this. When he sees us upset with our failures, he launches himself against us. In our heart he insinuates feelings of despair, more weighty than lead. If we entertain these feelings, their very weight drags us down; we break free from the chain which held us, and we swirl into the depths of the abyss."[63]

All too often, alas, experience bears out those last few words. The majority of falls that have not been atoned for, which have caused scandal in the Church, and the greater part of those which only the angels of peace know about and weep for, proceed from discouragement. Without discouragement, with trusting reparation, nothing would have been lost. But after a fall, which in many cases is only a surprise, the demon of despair begins to tempt the disconcerted soul, wielding arguments that get ever more discouraging. These conclude in that crushing thought which came to Cain: *My punishment is greater than I can bear* (Gen 4: 13).

From that moment on, as St. Paul warns us, the prince of darkness becomes lord of the soul. He directs it; he pushes it around and drops it wherever he likes, *operatur in filios diffidentiae—he is at work in the sons of disobedience* (Eph 2: 2). He has communicated two of his more diabolical dispositions to the soul—distancing itself from God by sin, and the fear of God through hopelessness. And let us not be led to believe that this temptation arises only after coarse faults have been committed. The Spirit of Deceit also knows how to use this weapon—the more terrible when it is easily concealed—against the virtuous souls after trivial faults. And if he does manage to lead it to total despair, the least he does is to paralyze the soul on its way to virtue, to disconcert it, to weaken its more powerful efforts, and freeze its fervor. Thus the soul is led to melancholy and discouragement; everything is "turned turtle," no care is now put into making reparation for faults, and the result is lukewarmness, with its almost irreparable harm.

Has God's mercy been abused?

Our faults, our habitual faults above all, offer Satan an easy means to achieve this result. It certainly may be observed that it is in his fight against the virtue of hope that the infernal spirit tries hardest *to disguise himself as an angel of light* (2 Cor 11: 14). It is not difficult for him to fulfill this role by contrasting our innumerable infidelities with the invitation of grace, our ingratitude with divine goodness, our failures with our resolution. It is in dismay that the soul exclaims: "Isn't it understandable that God gets tired and shuts off the fountain of help that I am abusing? With good reason he abandons me! Now is the moment to decide against making an effort, because my repeated failures have shown themselves to be superior to my strength. I had presumed excessively on God and on myself. Why should I expend my sterile efforts day after day if I am never to achieve a holiness which is impossible? My experience has plainly shown that with my weakness such heights are not within my reach. For how long am I going to continue making resolutions—*quandiu ponam consilia in anima mea,* with no result other than feeling the sorrow of failing in them throughout the day—*dolorem in corde meo per diem,* and to give the enemy a reason for cheering at my faults, *usque exaltabitur inimicus meus super me* (see Ps 13: 2–3)?

"Despairing soul: what gives joy to the enemy are not so much your faults as the depression and the distrust in the mercy of God they produce in you. 'This,' says Father

Colombière, 'is the greatest evil that can come over a creature. While one is able to fight against this evil, there is nothing that cannot be converted into good and from which some advantage cannot be gained. . . . All the bad things you have done are as nothing when compared with what you do if you lack confidence. Hope until the end. I command this with all the power you have given me over you. If you obey me on this point, I will be responsible for your conversion.' "[64]

Weakness is no great evil

If, in the past, these pieces of advice were opportune, they are much more relevant nowadays. "This is the era of the dejected and the discouraged." And this evil, which paralyzes so many noble characters and such true intentions in the political and social fields, gives rise to even more havoc in souls, even in those who wish to please our Lord. "Happily," says St. Augustine, "divine Wisdom possesses the secret of offering men the opportune remedies according to the circumstances in which they find themselves."[65]

While the despairing and pessimist doctrines of Jansenism abounded in the seventeenth century, Wisdom brought St. Francis de Sales to life and made him speak and write. She crowned him Doctor of the universal Church at a moment of greatest dejection in an unhappy century.

Father Faber says that among all the gentle doctrines taught by the inspired St. Francis de Sales, none is more precious than that referring to the way we should consider and judge our own defects.[66]

St. Francis forbids, above all, losing one's balance when one has made a mistake, whatever it be. "One should die rather than consciously and deliberately offend God.

But if we do fall, we should try to be prepared to do everything before losing enthusiasm, hope, and resolve." [67] "If it occurs to you to commit some fault, do not lose courage. Rise up immediately as if you had not fallen." [68] "To be a good servant of God is to be charitable with one's neighbor; it is to have in the higher region of the soul an unflinching commitment to do the will of God, to have great humility and simplicity in abandoning oneself into his arms, and rising no matter how often one falls. It is to be patient with one's own defects and to bear the imperfections of others." [69] "Weakness is not a great evil, and there is great value in raising oneself little by little. I exhort you to do this." [70]

"It is important that in no way should you get dejected. But with patient courage you should embark calmly and with care on the task of curing your soul of the injuries it has received in the attacks." [71] "It is necessary, beloved daughters, to be very generous . . . and to be courageous enough to despise our evil inclinations, our ill-humor, our sensitivities and eccentricities, continually doing mortifications on those points and at every occasion. If, in spite of everything, some fault does get the better of us, let us not be checked. Let us raise our morale to be more faithful on the following occasion, and thus we progress on our journey toward God with a spirit of self-denial." [72]

"It is necessary to have an unyielding approach that does not tire of ourselves, because we will always have something to rectify or to sever. . . . Have you observed what those who are trying to mount a horse do? Although they fall frequently, they don't lose heart. For it is one thing to see oneself sometimes on the ground, but quite another to consider oneself defeated forever." [73]

"The distrust you feel toward yourself is good, provided that you use it as a basis for the confidence you ought to have in God. But if, at times, you are carried to dejection, to disquiet, disgust, or melancholy, I entreat you to reject it as the greatest of temptations. Never permit your spirit to dialogue with or to rebel in favor of a disquiet or dispirited heart, to which you may be inclined . . . , not even on the false pretext of humility." [74]

A paradox

We have now caught a glimpse of how St. Francis de Sales tackles discouragement by directly attacking its causes. Why do we get depressed? Because we exaggerate our weakness or because we do not recognize divine mercy. And most of the time, it is the two together. It may be said in passing that in this there occurs a strange but frequent phenomenon. The sinner falls from having ignored his own weakness and from having exaggerated God's mercy. After the fall, these two sentiments are reborn, but in reverse. Weakness acquires excessive proportions in one's eyes; it envelops the soul in what seems a mantle of sadness and confusion. The soul feels crushed. On the other hand, God, whom one had earlier offended with the greatest of ease on the assumption of an easily available pardon, now appears to be an unremitting avenger. The guilty soul fears him and is ashamed of itself. If she does not react against these disastrous temptations, she will in a cowardly way give up the fight. Instead of breaking off the ties with sin, she will give in to them without putting up any resistance. This is discouragement: the capitulation of the will, the tendency to do the opposite of what one ought to do—its fatal result is more frequent than final impenitence.

Our holy Doctor takes care to cure these two dispositions leading to discouragement by tackling what opposes them. He makes the soul seeking to sanctify itself understand that the journey embarked upon is long and arduous. Compared with the difficulties along the way, one's strength is woefully short. But at the same time he makes him see that *everything is possible in Him who comforts him*, equally after the fall as before it. He points out that God's heart is quick and generous to forgive and, at the same time, that God extends a strong arm to offer one support.

"Loneliness has its attacks; the world has its dangers. A positive outlook is needed everywhere, because Heaven is disposed to offering help in every corner of the world to anyone who has confidence in God, to anyone who implores his paternal assistance with humility and meekness."[75]

"You should renew all the resolutions you have made until now. Even though you see that in spite of these you continue to be entangled with your imperfections, do not stop seeking improvement, but look for God's help to support you. Throughout your life you will be imperfect and have much to put right. So you have to learn not to get tired of this exercise."[76]

"Maintain peace. . . . When it happens that, because of a surge of self-love and of passions, we have faltered with the laws of indifference toward those things which do not matter, let us turn our heart toward God as soon as we can. Let us say to him with a spirit of confidence and humility: *Be gracious to me, O Lord, for I am languishing* (Ps 6: 2). We set sail in peace and tranquillity; we take up the thread of our indifference and continue at our work. When we discover that the lute is out of tune, it isn't necessary to break its strings and throw it out! What we have to do is to lend an attentive ear to discover which is the discordant string, and then tighten or loosen it as required."[77]

"When you see how high the mountain of Christian perfection is, I hear you exclaim, 'My God! How am I going to climb it?' Courage, Philothea! When baby bees begin to take form, they are called nymphs; they cannot as yet fly among the flowers on the mountains and hill-sides to gather the nectar. They nourish themselves on what the mother bees have collected. Little by little, the nymphs grow wings and gain in strength. Soon they are able to fly over the countryside to gather it. It is that we are still like baby bees in devotion, and we are not able to fly high to the place we want to get to—which is none other than the summit of perfection. But as our desires and our resolutions begin to form, they will begin to grow wings for us, and one day, like spiritual bees, we will fly aloft. Meanwhile, let us feed on the nectar found in works of instruction that devout people from the past have left us. Let us pray to God to give us 'wings like a dove' not only to fly upward during the time of our present life but also to find repose in the eternity that is to come."[78]

"The job is never done. One has to return to it again and again with a healthy willingness. *When a man has finished,* Scripture says, *he is just beginning* (Sir 18:7). What we have done to date is good; but what we are about to embark on is better. And when we think we have finished, we will begin something else even better, and then another, until we depart from this life to begin another, which will have no end, because nothing better could be made to happen for us. Examine, then, beloved Mother, whether we ought to cry when such a great task weighs on our soul, and if one needs courage to keep going forward always. It is important never to pause. Examine and see what one has to cut out, since we have to apply the words: *the word of God is sharper than any two-edged sword, piercing to the division of soul and spirit, of joints and marrow* (Heb 4: 12)."[79]

"It is a real pity that simply having a desire for perfection is not sufficient to have it in fact; one may have to attain it by the sweat of one's brow and the effort of work. You may say to me: 'We are so imperfect!' It will be like that. But do not be discouraged by this thought. Don't think you are going to be able to live without imperfections, because it is not possible while we are in this world. What is important is that you do not love them or give them shelter in your heart. That is to say, that you do not willingly commit them and that you do not wish to co-exist with them. If you meet these conditions, you will be able to maintain peace and will not be bewildered by the perfection you aim to achieve. It is enough for you to have it at death. Do not be timid. Walk firmly along God's path. You are armed with a soul of faith, and nothing can damage you."[80]

"In this enterprise (which is the purification of the soul), Philothea, we must have courage and patience. There are souls who, after starting to be devout for a while, realize that they are still subject to many imperfections. They begin to be dissatisfied, disturbed, and discouraged, and they almost let their hearts give in to the temptation to give up everything and go back to their old way of life. . . . What a pity it is to see such souls! It is good for our humility for us to be wounded in this spiritual warfare. But we are never defeated, unless we lose courage or our life. Imperfections and venial sins cannot deprive us of spiritual life; this is lost only by mortal sin. So, it only remains for us not to lose courage. *Save me, O Lord, from cowardice and discouragement*, David says. Fortunately for us, in this war we are always victorious, provided that we are willing to fight."[81]

No reason to lack confidence in God

We have to recognize that in all these teachings St. Francis de Sales was speaking to souls who were more or less advanced along the way of perfection. The faults to which he refers, which should not discourage them, were usually venial sins or imperfections. Nonetheless, more blameworthy souls are not excluded from this piece of advice. He addresses all souls, no matter how great their failures may have been, when he adds: "Feed your soul with a filial confidence in God. In the same measure in which you find yourself replete with imperfections and weaknesses, lift up your heart to regain hope." [82]

"After falling we ought to say with our heart: 'My friend, take courage in the name of God; let us tread with care; let us ask our God for help.' " [83]

"Provided there is no desire to remain or to fall asleep in evil, falls into mortal sin do not impede the progress that has been made through devotion. Although this progress is lost by sinning mortally, one recovers it with the first repentance for this sin—provided, as I have said, one has not remained a long time in the state of sin. . . . And in no way should one be discouraged. With holy humility, on the contrary, one should recognize one's illness, accuse oneself, seek forgiveness, and invoke aid from Heaven." [84]

Let us pause to reflect on the first phrase of this last quotation. Grave falls, if they are not followed by languishing in evil (that is to say, they have not become a habit), not only do not leave a stain after their forgiveness, but they do not even prevent the soul from immediately recovering the ground it had earlier conquered through devotion and struggle. The sin was undoubtedly a setback, a step backward; but absolution and perfect contrition compensate for this loss and make good the damage.

But what if we did remain immersed in sin for a while and languished in evil? Clearly, as the detention was greater and the slippage larger, the losses will be greater—but not irreparable. According to holy writ, the earlier merits will be reborn with forgiveness: *None of the transgressions which he has committed shall be remembered against him; for the righteousness that he has done he shall live* (Ezek 18: 22). Thus our Saint concludes: "There is no reason to lack confidence, for however miserable one may be, God is merciful toward those who truly want to love him and who have placed all their hope in him." [85]

Hope and fear

These thoughts will be developed further in the second half of this book. There our Doctor will make use of the same view of our faults to lead us to redouble our confidence in divine mercy. For the moment, these thoughts are enough to shut the gate on despair, and to show that the fear inspired by the knowledge of our weakness ought always to be sober and dominated by an unshakeable confidence in God. Our Saint insists in a particular way on the need for and on the way to combine these two dispositions. "There will always be a fight between fear and hope, but take into account that hope always will be the stronger, given the omnipotence of the One who lends us a hand." [86]

" 'Do penance,' says St. John, which is to say: level the mountains of pride, fill in the valleys of lukewarmness and pusillanimity, for salvation is at hand (see Lk 3: 5). The valleys which the evangelist refers to are fear, when the dejection we feel is exaggerated. Viewing the great faults we have committed brings with it a certain horror, an astonishment, and a fear that attacks the heart. These are the valleys that one has to fill with confidence and with hope, in preparation for the coming of our Lord.

Speaking one day to a saintly woman, a penitent who had committed great sins, a saint said: 'Have fear—but hope!' Fear so that you do not fall into pride; but hope so as not to fall into despair or to become discouraged. For hope without fear is presumption. Every valley shall be filled—*omnis vallis implebitis*. With confidence and with fear we should fill those valleys of discouragement which were formed when we got to know our sins." [87]

The devil confesses

It seems as though St. Francis de Sales, even after his death, wished to continue his campaign against despair. For he wrenched out a confession from the devil that provides great solace to the most criminal of souls.

A young person from Chablais had been possessed by an evil spirit for five years. During the process of beatification of our Saint, she was being taken to the bishop of Geneva. As he was not free to see her for a few days, Monsignor Charles Auguste de Sales and the Mother of Changey questioned her beside the mortal remains of the Saint. An eyewitness testifies[88] that during one of these sessions, the devil raised his screams to ever greater heights, saying: "Why do I have to come out?" To which the Mother of Changey fervently invoked: "Mother of God, pray for us! Mary, Mother of Jesus, come to our aid!" Hearing these words, the infernal spirit redoubled his shrieks and yelled: 'Mary, Mary. For me there is no Mary! Do not utter that name, for it makes me tremble. If there was a Mary for me as there is for you, I would not be what I am. But for me there is no Mary!"

All those present wept. The devil repeated: "If only I

had a single instant of the many you waste. Just one moment and a Mary, and I would not be a devil."

We who live have the present moment to return to God, and to Mary who can obtain the grace for us. Who, then, can despair?

Part II

4

Humility through Self-Knowledge

Three benefits

Let us not get discouraged or be surprised at our failures, for they are simply unavoidable. At the same time they are extremely salutary. This, however, is only the negative side of the art of using one's faults. It is time, now, to consider the positive side. At the school of St. Francis de Sales we learn how our sins can be used to our spiritual advantage, without losing an iota of their ugliness and malice.

This advantage will obviously not come from our sins themselves but from the mercy of God and the grace of Christ. God knows how to make our iniquities serve his goodness and to turn around our weakness to our salvation. Manure is nothing but rottenness. And yet, as St. Bernard observes: "A farmer and a gardener use it to make the earth produce better and more abundant fruits. In the same way, God makes use of our imperfections to produce within our souls numerous fruits of virtues. God's goodness can always make use of our wills and dissolute actions to help the beauty of his divine plan. So he condescends to use our imperfections for our advantage." [89]

For a number of reasons, this advantage is very important. On the one hand, it will make us have a greater hatred and an unrelenting hostility toward our mistakes.

On the other hand, by permitting these faults for our good, God will be associating us with his divine plan.

We should cooperate with the Redeemer's plans as revealed to us by the Church. We should combat Satan with his own weapons, turn his artifices back on him, and transform into a medicine the very wounds he inflicts on us.[90] In this way, we will vindicate St. John Chrysostom's observation: "Often the devil himself is very useful to us provided we make him act for our good."[91]

Quoting St. Paul, St. Augustine sums up this advantage in three words: *Omnia in bonum* (*All things work for the good of those who love God*). Yes, everything, even our failures. Because one then gets up and is more *humble*, more *careful*, and more *fervent*."[92]

In this regard St. Francis de Sales cries out: "Dear imperfections, you make us accept our misery, practice both humility and contempt of ourselves, as well as patience and diligence."[93]

Humility

Let us now consider the first of these advantages, humility. After St. Augustine, the saintly bishop of Geneva is the first person to point this out.

"Your Ladyship, may the Holy Spirit be pleased to inspire me with words to write to you. To live a devout life constantly, we should sow powerful and excellent maxims in our mind.

"The first maxim I recommend for your consideration is the one given by St. Paul: *In everything God works for good with those who love him* (Rom 8:28). And truly speaking, since God can and knows how to draw good from evil, will he not do so for those who have given themselves completely to him? Yes, even these sins (and may God forbid us from committing them) can be converted into good, by his providence, for his own people. If David had not sinned, he would never have been so overwhelmed with humility."[94]

"We should, of course, hate our defects—but peacefully and serenely. Our hatred should not be revengeful and spiteful. We should face them courageously and profit from them by a holy contempt of ourselves. If this contempt is lacking, then your imperfections, perceived by you so subtly, are only further strengthened. And nothing is more conducive to retaining our faults than our uneasiness and hurry to get rid of them."[95]

If there is one torment here on earth that souls, zealous for their perfection, suffer from, it is the twofold sentiment of the need for humility and the problems that arise from this need. On the one hand, this virtue, a necessity for man in this mortal life, is the support and foundation of all virtues.[96] It also "is the mother, the root, the nurse, and the fulcrum of every other virtue."[97] On the other hand, when it seems that this virtue is about to germinate spontaneously and blossom in the infected soil of our miserable heart, what does it discover there better embedded than itself? Pride alone, *the beginning of every other sin,*[98] which incessantly seeks to stifle it.

The ingenuity and versatility of the devil's skills are seen best in his drive and astuteness. He is truly a snake who makes himself "born" in us and grows faster than we do. He would love to entangle us in his evil designs and to poison, with his venom, our most saintly and ordinary actions, including our most secret and best intentions. "Our very virtues nourish him. He prospers by seeking to appropriate for his own benefit God's most exquisite gifts."[99] If he gives the impression of relenting, it is merely to spread out his tentacles, at his convenience, into our disillusioned souls. Finally, according to St.

Francis de Sales, "pride is such a widespread evil among men that we can never sufficiently stress the necessity of persevering in the practice of this very holy and lovable virtue of humility." [100]

Let no one consider himself sufficiently strong to face the enemy of such an indispensable virtue. Because it is not within our power to destroy him in this life, we should, at least, eagerly make use of all means to weaken and neutralize his attacks. The most effective of these means is offered to us precisely by our faults. In the hands of Samson, the dried jawbone of an animal became a lethal weapon against the Philistines. So too our sins, however hideous they be, can be transformed into an all-powerful sledgehammer against pride. In this way, they become an opportunity for our salvation and perfection.

In fact, if pride is an inordinate esteem and love of our so-called excellence, then, according to our lovable Saint, humility is the "true knowledge and voluntary recognition of our misery." [101] What can be more suitable to bring about within us this true knowledge, if not the sight of our faults? Truly they are, according to the clever expression of Father Alvarez, the many windows through which the light enters in great abundance to shine on our misery. Originating in men, they are more effective than humiliations; they illuminate the most intimate vital forces of the soul and convince it of its nothingness. And, adds St. Francis de Sales, "this knowledge of our nothingness should not disturb but rather make us more gentle to humble ourselves as poor and miserable." [102]

" 'But I'm so miserable,' you will say, 'so full of imperfections.' Do you have complete knowledge of them? Yes? If so, thank God that he gave you this knowledge, and don't weep over it so much. You should indeed be happy to know that you are nothing but misery itself." [103]

"One must accept the truth that we are poor and can do hardly anything." [104]

" 'I want to tell you that you will remain faithful if you are humble.'

" 'But will I be humble?'

" 'Yes, if you want to be.'

" 'Yes, I want to be.'

" 'Therefore you are humble.'

" 'But I truly feel that I am not.'

" 'So much the better. For this attitude will definitely help you to be so.' " [105]

"The limitations we experience in carrying on our external work and internal affairs are very much a part of humility. And humility in its turn begets and sustains generosity." [106]

In fact, how can we have self-confidence and consider ourselves to be of some importance if, at the first sign of temptation, we get completely upset? At that moment, our resolutions falter and fade away *like a spark or like a used rope thrown into the fire* (see Is 1:31). How the memory of the reality of our misery weakens our pride! It is only then that humility can set up its abode in the truth. Should not one expect to hear a voice cry out: *May your judgments be upright.*[107] *Behold, you have been weighed in the balances and found wanting.*[108] Whereas *you considered yourself to be heavier, you are lighter.*[109]

The Good Shepherd

According to the holy Doctors, this is God's principal plan in permitting our sins. The Good Shepherd makes use of three kinds of staff for his sheep. One is the staff of correction: these are adversities. The second is the staff of trials: these are temptations. The third is the staff of indignation, which permits our sins. Each of the three forces man to recognize his nothingness and to humble himself. But the third is much more effective than the first two. It is here, in experiencing his failures, that he really becomes aware of his misery. As Jeremiah said, *I am a man who sees my poverty under the staff of the Lord's indignation.*[110] This staff is so salutary that God has no hesitation in using it on his best friends. Their very virtues could be a terrible obstacle to their humility. So he sometimes allows them to commit imperfections. Or else, he permits their old perverse inclinations to raise their heads so as to teach them, by experiencing their own frailty, never to rely on their own strength."[111]

"Our Lord," continues our Saint, "permits these small encounters to defeat us so that we remain humble. We are also reminded that it is divine assistance and not our strength that helps us overcome temptations."[112]

"Be patient. . . . If God allows you to stumble, it is only to bring home to you that if he did not support you, you would quickly fall."[113]

God has healed some people suddenly, without leaving any trace of their former sickness. In the case of Mary Magdalen, she was changed from a cesspool of corruption to a fountain of perfection and was never troubled again. But this very same God has also left in many of his cherished disciples, some time after their conversion, many traces of their evil inclinations; and all this for their greater good. Witness the blessed St. Peter, who, after his first call, stumbled several times into imperfections and once completely and very miserably collapsed through his denial.

"According to Solomon, a maidservant becomes unbearable if promoted, all of a sudden, to the position of mistress. So also there is a great danger for the soul that has all along been pampering its passions: it may become haughty and vain if it is suddenly given the complete responsibility of being a mistress. That is why it is better to overcome our imperfections gradually. Saintly men and women have taken several decades to do so."[114]

"Remain at peace and gently put up with your little troubles. Because you belong fully to God, he will guide you properly. If he does not free you very quickly from your imperfections, it is because he wants you to be freed of them in a more profitable way. He wants to train you for a longer period in humility so that you be rooted in this dear virtue."[115]

"You will recall that I have often said you should be as attached to practicing the virtue of fidelity to God as to practicing the virtue of humility. Your attachment to fidelity is seen by renewing your resolutions to serve the Divine Goodness as often as you break them, and by putting yourself on guard not to do so again. And your attachment to humility: by recognizing your small-mindedness when you break these resolutions."[116]

Patience with oneself

"Those aspiring to the pure love of God don't need to be as patient with others as with themselves. One has to bear with one's imperfections in order to attain perfection. I am saying: bear it with patience and do not love or caress it. This suffering nurtures the practice of humility."[117]

Let us bear in mind that this doctrine of our Saint, as well as of other Doctors, is applicable not only to small imperfections. St. Isidore and St. Thomas[118] state that God sometimes permits our falling into serious faults in order to punish in some way our pride. The gravity of these sins, they say, is less serious than the sin of pride; and the divine mercy makes use of them to terrify, shake up, and call the proud soul to heel. He is like a skillful doctor, who, in order to heal a more serious infirmity, often allows his patient to fall into the clutches of a more painful yet less dangerous sickness. Louis Veuilot has aptly written: "It is a grace granted to man's miserable state that he falls sometimes, when stronger feet could have carried him to the peaks of pride." St. John Chrysostom makes similar observations: "God sometimes permits the sins of noble and great souls to be made known. Through their faults, the Lord seeks to strip them of that popular glory for which they have faced every possible danger. He shows them to be as ephemeral as the flowers in the field. He brings them to consecrate themselves unreservedly to him and to consider him the only end of all their actions." [119]

He points out some illustrious penitents, who, by meditating on God's blessings and recalling their minor imperfections, were filled with repentance. The saintly bishop of Constantinople again adds: "And yet these medicines are not enough for us. To overcome our pride, we need some other force. Which one?—The multitude of our sins and the perversity of our conscience that still dares to leave us elated even after having sunk us into a thousand ignominies." [120]

This is the language used by several other Fathers of the Church. St. Augustine states emphatically: "God prefers to look at bad actions accompanied by humility than at godly works infected with pride." [121] According to St. Optat of Mileve, "Sins accompanied with humility are worth more than innocence with pride." [122]

For St. Gregory of Nyssa, "a cartload of good works drawn by pride leads to Hell, whereas a cartload of sins drawn by humility leads to Paradise." And for St. Gregory the Great: "It often happens that he who sees himself in God's presence covered with stains is nevertheless, because of an accompanying deeper humility, more richly adorned."

And finally, St. Bernard concludes his beautiful justification of virginity and humility saying: "The sinner who has chosen the path of humility to walk in the footsteps of the Lamb has taken a surer path than the man who, though preserving his chastity, follows the path of pride. For the humility of the former purifies him from his blemishes, while the pride of the latter cannot but blemish his purity." [123]

We hope to be excused for so many quotations. The subject, however, is so important and delicate that it is necessary for us to have the backing of powerful authoritative persons. Besides, we will not find in these texts a shadow of exaggeration if we meditate on what St. Thomas says in the *Summa* (q. 16, art. 6): "Pride is by nature the worst of all the sins, graver than infidelity, despair, homicide, lust, etc." The reason for this, he continues, is its hatred for God. In the case of other sins, man turns away from God through ignorance, or weakness, or through a desire for some other good. But pride turns away from God solely because it refuses to accept God and his Law. That is why, while all the other vices flee God's presence, pride alone dares to face him. Hence the words: *God opposes the proud* (Jas 4: 6). To detest God and his commandments is nothing but the consequence of the other sins. And this detestation belongs to the very nature of pride, whose very act is a despising of God. Now, that which subsists by virtue of its own power takes precedence over that which exists by virtue of something else. It follows that pride, by its very nature, is the gravest of all sins and constitutes their formal malice.

"If we cannot acquire many virtues," St. Jeanne Françoise de Chantal used to say, "then let us at least have humility." It is precisely by the sincere acknowledgment of our lack of virtues, that is to say, by the true notion of our spiritual poverty and our nothingness, made known to us by our faults, that we can install in our hearts the mother virtue of all other virtues. One cannot but cry out with our lovable Saint: "Dear imperfections, you make us acknowledge our misery and make us practice humility!" How can one but not apply the *Felix culpa, O happy fault!* to each of our failures?

"While deploring the havoc caused by a flood, would you not rejoice," wrote a saintly Daughter of the Visitation, "if it had deposited, on your property, excellent stones to be used as the foundation of a palace you wanted to build? Now, humility is called upon to be the foundation of the spiritual edifice. For God, who alone has the right to build, as the Prophet said (Ps 126: 1), will never build except on the foundations that our self-knowledge has dug out for us." [124]

Isn't it through our faults that we can dig deeper foundations and attain with greater certainty this salutary knowledge of ourselves? Piece by piece, these faults dismantle the imaginary scaffolding of our own strength. Let us not put off seeing ourselves supported by divine mercy alone in the abyss of our nothingness. What a precious discovery! God expects it. *He regards the humility* of his servants. As much as He opposes *the proud,* He gives his graces to *the humble.*[125] According to St. Augustine, this grace loves to flow in the most lowly valleys, and floods us in proportion to our humiliation. And, in the depths of our acknowledged nothingness, it lays the foundations of true holiness. Henceforth, this foundation is better protected against the onslaught of pride. If vanity still seeks an entry into this new edifice, just one word will suffice to drive it off: *Peccavi* (I have sinned).[126] This is my work, all the rest is God's. To quote the example of an eminent successor of St. Francis de Sales: "I will use the memory of my past failures to prepare a secret book that I will name *Cure for pride* and whose pages I will read over and again. They will exude the odor of my nothingness and poison the worm of my pride." [127]

The higher God raises me, be it with St. Paul to the third heaven, the more will I discover, through imitating his Apostles in the recollections of my previous infidelities, a counterweight to heavenly favors. This will keep me in a just contempt of myself. I will thus be complying with the counsel of the Holy Spirit: *In the day of prosperity, adversity is not to be forgotten.*[128]

In St. Gertrude's life we see that God permitted several spiritual weaknesses to safeguard her humility. This situation distressed the servant of God. A devout lady, sensitive to her entreaties, kept praying for her for quite some time. One day, our Lord told this lady: "These imperfections of which my beloved is complaining are very useful for her. Every day I fill her soul with such an abundance of graces that in order to protect her from attacks of vanity I am forced to hide a number of them behind a cloud of these small shortcomings. Just as manure fertilizes the earth, the sentiment that a soul has of its infirmity germinates gratitude within her; and every time she is humbled by her faults I grant her the grace that destroys them. Gradually, I transform the imperfections into virtues. One day the soul will be surprised to see everything in a clear, shadowless light." [129]

Gratitude toward God

Gratitude toward God is another fruit that can *be made to germinate* by the perception of our shortcomings. Humility is, basically, truth. While it unveils to us "the nothingness from which we have been extracted, it shows in better light the good within us that comes from God as from its primary cause." [130] Hence, the more humility illuminates the soul as to its misery, the more it spreads before our eyes, in resplendent brightness and by overwhelming contrast, the magnitude and multiplicity of divine favors. This makes it easier for us to be grateful to *the author of every perfect gift* (Jas 1: 17).

This is not the least of the benefits that we can extract from our faults. Ingratitude, the offspring of pride, "is a common sin that reaches out to all the rest and makes them infinitely more enormous." [131] It is a hot wind that dries up the fountain of grace. The only way this vice can be victoriously overcome is through the consideration of our infidelities in relation to God's persistent mercy.

"Certainly, in the presence of God's mercy, nothing can so effectively humble us as the multitude of his benefits; nothing can be so deeply humiliating for us, in the presence of his justice, as the multitude of our misdeeds against him. Let us consider what he has done for us and how we have acted against him. As we reflect on our sins, one by one, let us also consider minutely his graces. We should not fear that the knowledge of his gifts will make us proud—provided we also remember the truth that whatever is good in us is not of our making. Do mules, just because they are loaded with the precious perfumed furniture of the prince, lose their stupidity and their stubbornness? What good do we possess that we have not received? And if we have received it, why do we glory in it? On the contrary, the vivid realization of graces received makes us humble. For knowledge begets gratitude. However, if, at the sight of God's graces conferred on us, some sort of vanity should make us proud, then the infallible cure is to resort to the consideration of our ingratitude, our imperfections, and our misery. If we reflect only on how we acted when God was not with us, we will understand very well that what we do when he is with us is not the result of our own effort. Possessing it will allow us to enjoy it as well as rejoice in it. But now we will glorify God alone because he is its author." [132]

"Fill your memory with the recollection of your faults and infidelities in order to humble and improve yourself; recall the benefits received from God in order to thank him for them." [133]

"Tell your heart: O, my heart! Don't any more be unfaithful, ungrateful, and disloyal toward this great benefactor. And how can my heart, henceforth, be no more subservient to God, who has brought about so many wonders and graces in my life!" [134]

Being understanding with others

Finally, St. Francis de Sales hopes that the light projected by our faults and our weakness will help us, through humility, to be indulgent with the weakness of others.

"Humility," he says, "prevents us from being troubled by our imperfections when we remember those of others. For why should we be more perfect than others? It also prevents us from being unduly disturbed by the faults of others when we recall our own. Why should we find it unusual that others have imperfections when we, ourselves, have so many?" [135]

St. John Chrysostom, with his customary forcefulness, emphasizes this much-unrecognized effect of God's plan that our faults should procure for us. He goes on to suggest the reason why the priesthood was not entrusted to the angels: there was the fear that, inasmuch as it was impossible for them to sin, they would be very severe and call down thunder and lightning on sinners. Men, on the other hand, having experience of human frailty, would be naturally more understanding when they see sin in others.

It is for this reason, continues the saintly bishop, that in the past, as today, God has permitted those in the Church who are the trustees of his authority, to make mistakes: the recollection of their failures makes them more human toward their brethren. He illustrates this point with two examples, one from the New Testament and the other from the Old Testament. St. John Chrysostom places before us the ardent, intrepid, St. Peter, who never thought that he could be scandalized or ashamed of his Master. He swore his loyalty to him three times—then denied him miserably, not under the threat of torture or death, but faced with the accusation of a maid-servant! Chrysostom then considers the Prophet Elijah: his impetuous zeal overthrew battalions and reduced an entire population to a state of famine. But, shortly afterward, he became terrified and bewildered, and took to his heels in the presence of an angry woman named Jezabel. "God," he concludes, "permitted the fall of Peter, pillar of the Church, haven of the faith, universal doctor, in order to teach him to treat others with mercy. And Elijah also fell, with God's permission, so that he might put on the cloak of charity and become indulgent like his Lord." [136]

St. Bernard takes up this question again by commenting on the proverb: "He who is well does not notice another's sickness; and he who is satiated does not understand the suffering of the hungry." The more a sick person resembles another sick person, and one hungry person another hungry person, the deeper is their sympathy for the other's difficulties. In order to feel the unhappiness of others, one should have experienced it personally. It is only through knowledge of ourselves that we will be capable of recognizing our neighbor's soul as our own and, thereby, come to his aid.[137]

Let us apply these lessons to ourselves. So long as we are standing up, we will be unable to excuse or to understand others' failings that scandalize, irritate, or disgust us. And how many times it is nothing else but a secret pride, under the garb of zeal, that angers us? However, just let a similar fault floor us—and very quickly our severity will turn to compassion. Then will we understand St. Augustine's saying: "Any sin possible to man can stain my soul"; as well as that of the *Imitation of Christ*: "We are all weak, but consider yourself the weakest of all."[138]

5

Getting to Love Our Misery

Humility

"Humility in its highest form," according to St. Francis de Sales, "is not merely the voluntary admission of our misery. We should also love it and delight in its possession." Why? "Not because we are wanting in generosity and courage. But, rather, because through humility we can all the more glorify the majesty of God and, in addition, hold our neighbor in greater esteem than ourselves." [139]

For St. Magdalen of Pazzi, "humility is a continuous recognition of our nothingness as well as a feeling of contentment in the midst of whatever brings us shame." This is the peak that our faults can and should help us to reach. They throw light on and expose our misery, which we should not only accept but also love.

Our amiable Doctor says that "we are all capable of committing the same faults we see in others. This should not surprise us. Although for some time we may succeed in avoiding them, it won't be long before we ourselves commit some serious faults. These should be used to our advantage because of the very ignominy they lend." [140]

"If we could be pleasing to God whether we were full of imperfections or not, what would be our choice? Would we not rather choose to remain imperfect? In this way we would be able to foster this saintly virtue of humility." [141]

An illustrious Christian was of the opinion that "to acknowledge and take pleasure in our misery is a sign of God's great mercy. Through the virtue of humility, God draws our salvation out of damnation. At the same time, he makes our sins themselves glorify him. Once enlightened, the soul accepts to remain seated on the dunghill of its miseries, adorned with humiliation. In this way, it resembles Job, submerged by his sufferings. The misery and ignominy that a soul suffers because of its serious falls should rather be taken as enriching treasures. Unfortunately, this happiness is not experienced by most men, for it remains hidden from their view. They stay impoverished, ignorant of the wealth hidden in their own forest. They are unable to possess it, as they don't know how to search for it." [142]

An eminent nun of the Visitation Order spoke eloquently of this treasure: "Our faults and ignominy are a large part of our resources. And the woof of these resources is the love begotten by this ignominy. To try to weave without a woof would result in gaping holes. Similarly, it is a sign of the devil's work if, instead of loving our humiliations, we get agitated and disturbed by them. We should profit from our faults. Seeing something good in our failures will make up for our lack of willpower to act and put ourselves on the road to progress. Life is a series of falls; after each fall, we should immediately get up and say: 'I will not make this mistake again.' If we approach our failures in this spirit, they will not be harmful; we will give ourselves light, strength, and encouragement. And whatever we have lost through cowardice will be recovered by humility." [143]

Indeed, the truth is that we are miserable. If it were not for God's gifts, we would be only nothingness and sin. Let us joyfully recognize this truth and, provided no scandal is given, help our neighbors to do so, too. One can also cite the example of a man in love with science, who, thrilled after discovering a scientific truth, does his best to prove it and make it acceptable to his peers. If we don't have this attitude, it would amount to disloyalty and a lack of humility. We could then merit King David's reproach: *How long will you love vain words, and seek after lies?*[144] A saintly soul once exclaimed: "These blemishes suit me perfectly."

A true spiritual daughter of St. Francis de Sales, in her enthusiasm to apply the advice of her spiritual father, cried out: "If it were possible to sin without offending God, then I would wish to sin continuously in order to remain ceaselessly in a state of shame and nothingness." [145]

Joy in being nothing

The saintly bishop of Geneva adds that it is not only "out of respect for the truth" that humility inspires "joy in being nothing and in being reduced to nothing." [146] It is also, and above all, out of respect for the "humiliations suffered by the Word Incarnate." By clothing his adorable innocence with the raiment of sin, the Divine Lamb condescended to take on completely, with the exception of sin, our shattered human nature. The Gospels tell us of the depths of lowliness to which he descended, of his own will as well as of his great desire to be inebriated with indignation. Even centuries of meditation wouldn't suffice to make us realize fully his Sacred Heart's thirst for humiliation. This thirst is what goaded him on joyfully toward the bloody ignominies, as if to a sumptuous banquet, perfectly matching his status of "lord among sinners." The truly Christian soul feels a strong need to take part in this banquet at the side of her

Beloved. Indeed, being guilty, how can she allow him, the Innocent One, to drink all alone from the cup of humiliation. In this she also longs for her share. She looks forward to the happiness of putting her lips to the very spot where her God and her Savior placed his and where he transformed the bitterest gall into a delicious drink.

Judging by St. Bernard's observations, we should also include humiliations that are the indispensable means along the path of humility. Once the soul is convinced of the need of this virtue, it should love humiliations and look out for them, like the traveler who, keenly intent on reaching his destination, sticks to the road leading to it. Our misery, as we will consider in the next chapter, makes us lovable. For within us it attracts God's loving and abundant mercies.

Each of these topics offers us sufficient means to use our sins to foster within us a love for our misery. Our sins help us to see our misery in a better light. Their humiliating weight helps to balance, in a practical and satisfying manner, the shame they arouse with the inner and outer opprobrium we deserve. What our Savior accepted and eagerly sought out as the ransom for saving sinners will be appreciated as falling to our lot in strict proportion to our real state as sinners.

Each of our falls will now become one more milestone on the path, diminishing our self-esteem and selfish demands. We will move to occupy *the lowest place* (Lk 14: 10)—that is, indeed, the one most befitting us. But even here, unfortunately, our pride remains invincible and makes us feel superior to him who wanted to be the *last of all, the shame of men and the abjection of people* (Is 53; Ps 22).

The thermometer for holiness

Our faults can be of great benefit to us provided they help us to love our misery. Our beloved Saint makes humility the thermometer of holiness. He also accepts without hesitation that a soul through its faults can make greater progress than one less prone to fall. "Perhaps you see a sister repeatedly stumbling. And yet, it could happen that she is more virtuous and pleasing to God than another with a dozen natural or acquired virtues. We can explain it like this. The former despite all her imperfections remains courageous and does not get unduly upset or troubled at the sight of her weakness. The latter, however, because she makes less of an effort and works less, might well be less virtuous. Consequently, she would need less courage and be in possession of a lesser degree of humility than the former who appears to be weak. St. Peter had a large number of imperfections, and yet he was chosen to be the leader of the Apostles. In fact, even after receiving the Holy Spirit, he made a number of mistakes. But, despite his faults, at which he was never surprised, he was always a man of courage; and that is why our Lord made him his lieutenant. He was favored by Christ more than any of the others so that no one would ever have any reason to say that he didn't deserve to be ranked higher than St. John or the other Apostles." [147]

St. Jeanne de Chantal loved repeating the following teaching of her spiritual father. In a letter to Sister F. A. of the Cross, of Fesigny, we read: "My dearly beloved child, your discouragement is nothing but a temptation. Just tell me what good does it bring you? Are you motivated by it? Do you think it is in our power to be always aware of God and never make a mistake? In that case we would need to be angels. It is my earnest request that you learn to adjust yourself to life's miserable conditions without anxiety and worry. If you feel guilty of lacking in loyalty, just be humble about it without giving in to discouragement. If you cultivate and keep a relaxed and serene mind, the humiliation and love of your misery will be more pleasing to God than all your fussily faithful deeds." [148]

A rule of conduct

Our saintly Doctor wanted to point out to us occasions that would give us the chance to despise ourselves. He did so because he feared we might not otherwise give them due importance. And this even in situations when our faults are very doubtful. The most worthwhile stand to be taken, according to him, is the one that is most unfavorable to our pride and most favorable to holy humility.

"I would like to add," he writes, "a general rule of conduct to be applied in circumstances when we are not sure whether we have fulfilled our duty properly or whether we have offended God. In such a case, we should first of all remain humble, then ask God's forgiveness and pray for his light for the next time. Once this is done, we should completely forget what has happened and carry on with our usual work. For any thing done out of curiosity and haste to learn whether what we have done is correct or not undoubtedly has self-love for its source. This self-love wants us to know whether we are brave, just when the pure love of God says: 'How miserable and cowardly you have been.' Humble yourself. Put your trust in God's mercy, and always ask pardon for your mistakes. This done, set off once more on the path of your progress after taking a new resolve to be faithful." [149]

This is in keeping with the thinking of the author of the *Imitation*, who writes: "By trusting in your abounding mercy, Lord, I will more effectively obtain the forgiveness of my sins than by relying on the defence of my conscience by my justice." [150]

Witnesses to our weaknesses

Our faults manifest our misery and humility in a more evident way through being experienced than through being simply revealed in the hidden recesses of our soul. Our neighbor also is often a witness to our falls and sees plainly our weakness and misery. Consequently, to the shame from within is added shame from without. We ought to accept and love both forms and thereby double our spiritual gains. This is what was done by Mr. Bernières, a noble and pious soul to whom I have already referred. "You know," he wrote to a friend, "you are aware and a witness of my behavior when recently I was carried away. . . . That this incident took place in the presence of my friends consoles me. At least they will know what I am. Of course, I am unhappy that I displeased God and was not faithful in responding to his grace. And yet, in my humiliation, which I fully accept, I experience great joy. To be considered vile by others is a great happiness and also something pleasant for those who use it as a means of reparation for the ignominy suffered by God. From the knowledge of our imperfections, we grow in the conviction of our pure nothingness and extreme fragility. The recognition and sight of my misery have been useful in making evident so many truths! Indeed, it is true that I am merely nothing, weakness, corruption, and much less than I could ever imagine. And because of my love for truth, I continue to hold on to my nothingness. By my willing attachment to my nothingness I love and adore Divine Providence, who reveals it. I recognize and accept myself as miserable and yet feel at ease that everybody knows the truth and treats me accordingly."[151]

What better example of putting into practice the sublime teachings of the author of *Philothea*! And yet, St. Francis de Sales, known for his wise discretion, takes care to safeguard the demands of truth and charity. He protects truth when he discourages the mere simulation of mistakes as pretext to seek contempt for ourselves. (This excludes special cases of inspiration seen in the lives of the saints.) He further protects the claims of charity by recommending the amends to be made for any scandal or hurt feelings caused to our neighbor. "Suppose that, in a fit of anger or passion, I say something improper that is offensive to God and my neighbor; then I must repent and be extremely sorry for the offense. This will help me do my best to make amends for the offense committed. At the same time, however, I will accept the consequent abjection and contempt it has brought upon me. If we were able to separate one from the other, I would most vehemently reject sin, but humbly keep the abjection."[152] "I make some foolish mistake. Will it make me feel disgusted? For instance, I behave disgracefully and lose my temper inordinately. I express sorrow, on the one hand, for offending God, and, gladness, on the other, to be considered vile, abject, and miserable.

"Nevertheless, my daughter, pay careful heed to what I'm now going to tell you. Though we may love the abjection that results from the wrong done, we must, nevertheless, do all in our power to correct the mistake. I'll do my best to get the ulcer on my face removed, but if it remains, I will also love the scorn it brings me. The same rule must hold good in matters of sin. I flare up for this or that reason. This behavior hurts me, although I heartily welcome the abjection. And if we are to distinguish one from the other, then I will keep, affectionately, the abjection but reject the evil and sin." [153]

Suppose our attempts to make amends to our neighbor for our hurtful and scandalous behavior are successful. If we regain once more their high esteem as if nothing had ever happened, well, in that case, though we have the duty "to hide *our misery from their sight to prevent scandal*, we should rather hide it in the most intimate recesses of our heart for our own edification." [154]

Our Saint did not want anyone to be deprived of the advantage of abjection that comes from outside as long as it was in keeping with the dictates of charity and the duty of setting a good example.

"As for our faults . . . I wouldn't like you to take so much trouble to prevent them from surfacing. For their seriousness is not going to increase by merely being seen. Further, your hiding them is not going to make the sisters think that you don't have any imperfections. Or perhaps you think that their gravity increases because they appear in the open and have now been discovered or because they cause you greater embarrassment. Therefore, let us not be surprised or discouraged when we commit some imperfections in the presence of our sisters. Rather, we should be full of joy at being recognized as we really are." [155]

Someone in authority

When someone occupies a position of authority, he considers it important to protect his reputation as regards subordinates. Even in this situation, the founder of the Visitation Order would like one to profit from abjection wherever it is found. "You ask me . . . whether the Superior or Director might not react with a certain repugnance at her faults being noticed by the sisters or what she should tell a sister who, because of some judgment or thought, confesses to be imperfect. An example of this type could be, for instance, if someone felt that the Superior should have reacted less forcibly in making a reprimand.

"This is how the Superior should react in such a situation. She should consider lovingly her own misery. If the sister in question appeared disturbed during her confession, the Superior should appear to take no notice but change the trend of the conversation. In any case, she should keep the abjection within her heart. For one ought to be careful not to lose out of self-love any occasion for accepting our imperfect nature and for remaining humble. If, however, during her confession the sister concerned did not appear very disturbed, then it would be all right if the Superior were to let her know that she has slipped up. In this case it is true. Where the sister's judgment is incorrect, the Superior should say so, humbly. This should be done while still keeping the abjection as the treasure she deserves for having been misjudged as a defaulter.

"This little virtue of loving our shortcomings and misery, you see, should always be close to our heart. For we need it all the time, however advanced we are on the path of virtue; our sinful passions show up despite our closeness to God, and our great spiritual progress.

"The sisters should not be surprised at the Superior's mistakes. Even St. Peter, the pastor of Holy Church and Superior of all Christians, made a mistake and had to be corrected, as St. Paul relates (Gal 2: 11). Likewise, the Superior should not be surprised if anyone notices her shortcomings. Rather, let her imitate the humility and gentleness of St. Peter, who was ready to be corrected by St. Paul, his subordinate. In fact, it is difficult to say which is greater—Paul's courage in reprimanding Peter, or Peter's humility in accepting the reprimand for an action that was well intentioned." [156]

St. Mary Magdalen of Pazzi once came to know of the high esteem in which one of her novices held her. Weeping, she narrated her shortcomings and temptations. Picturing herself as the most criminal of human beings, she added: "I have told you all this to let you know what a criminal novice-mistress you have. If God had not shut me within a cloister, I would have been sentenced to life imprisonment or to the executioner's axe. So, please pray to God's boundless goodness for my salvation." [157]

Let us listen to a worthy daughter of St. Francis de Sales, nearer to us in time and distance. After being appointed Superior in her monastery, she told me this confidentially with regard to her Sisters. "What gratifies me is that my status of Superior exposes my shortcomings more easily. What is on a candle-stand is more visible than what is hidden in the obscurity of a cell." [158]

All the more, then, in the opinion of the bishop of Geneva, should someone privileged to occupy a lower position willingly embrace any humiliation coming from above. And he mercilessly chided anyone who was hypersensitive on this point:

" 'I get annoyed when I am despised.'

"The peacocks and monkeys act in this fashion.

" 'I rejoice in being despised.'

"This is the way the Apostles reacted. So you want to know how we should act when corrected and mortified? Consider mortification a precious fruit and hide it away in the heart. Then keep on fondling it kindly, in the most tender manner possible." [159]

Turning faults to our advantage

I hope that we have shown from the school of St. Francis de Sales all the advantages to be drawn from our faults by means of humility. In helping us to know our misery better, as well as love it, our faults can help us to rise from the depths they have lowered us to, to the highest degree of virtue. In this way they can be the source of a new luster for a soul. According to a text from Job (11: 17) and the thinking of St. Bernard, "The more abject the simple soul considers itself, by the recollection of its sins, the less abject will God consider it in his sight." [160]

Let us turn our faults to our advantage. According to Fénelon, our faults lower ourselves in our own esteem. And yet, he continues, they are more beneficial to us than our good works, despite the consolation the latter give us. "Faults are always faults. But in addition they embarrass us and bring about a return to God, doing an immense service.

"There are some substances that, outwardly, appear to dirty our garments but are, nevertheless, used to remove their stains. Similarly, the just, while detesting their sins, use them to purify their souls of pride, the greatest of sins." [161]

Let us learn to use our faults in the following way. The moment they escape us, let us remove all trace of them through penance. Let us make use of them also when their memory saddens us. Certain foul-smelling plants begin to give out a sweet fragrance when they begin to dry, and this change increases in proportion to their dryness. We should apply this example to the sins in our poor lives. A saintly daughter of the Visitation Order had preserved a paper bag with great joy. On her death, it was found in her cell with this inscription: "This is to perfume my heart with the precious smell of my misery." Into this packet she had put everything humiliating that had been said of or written about her: the defects that had been pointed out to her, whatever had been told to her very strongly by her confessor in her confessions, and all the faults on which she had received correction.[162]

It will not be worth our while to make such a packet. Alas! by just looking at our past life, we will see the bad plants of innumerable faults. We could use them to fill the packet and put them to our advantage in this way. Let us repeat the wonderful words of Father Colombière: "O Fortunate miseries that make me blush in the presence of God and humble myself before men! If you are that necessary for me, then I would not exchange you for the merits and virtues of others. I prefer being whatever is necessary to be humble. I give up all those graces that would deprive me of this advantage. In order never to lose this, I agree to be deprived of all the rest."

6

Confidence in God's Mercy

(i)

A duty to hope

Our misery becomes worthy of our love because it renders homage to the truth. It also makes it easier for us to imitate the Word made flesh. This truth will be understood more clearly if considered in relation to God's infinity.

St. Francis de Sales has already been quoted several times stating that our mistakes should not leave us with a feeling of helplessness and discouragement. The pain of having made these mistakes should always be coupled with a certain hidden confidence in divine goodness. The examples that we present to you will demonstrate how our sins and shortcomings, far from dampening our confidence, can be the source of our richest experiences.

The numerous passages of our Saint are clear enough and don't need any explanation. We will limit ourselves to reproducing them. But before doing so, it will not be a futile proposition to borrow some reflections from other sources, which are the synthesis and the theological proofs for this comforting doctrine.

First of all, let us hear Monsignor Gay present and develop the basic principles of this new aspect of the art of profiting from our faults. Quoting St. John, he says: "*God is love* (1 Jn 4: 8). God loves, and God loves us. He loves us because he is love itself. To exist, to love; and since we exist, to love us is one and the same thing for him, the one and only thing necessary. Isn't it therefore a duty for us all to have hope? Should we be so afraid of having too much hope? And so if we are always lacking in trust, can we be excused?

"One might say: But sin exists! Of course sin exists everywhere! And wherever it exists, it creates a problem. It becomes an obstacle to our progress, a problem for us, and creates complications. But can there be problems for God? Can one follow his path and yet create obstacles for him? He stops whenever he wishes, but only where he wishes to. He passes wherever it pleases him. The results of sin affect God in the sense that sin displeases him. But it never affects him in the sense that he changes because of it. It modifies his actions, but far from changing his essence it changes nothing of his primary and substantial disposition toward us—his love for us. As against our nothingness, we see his kindness turn to love. In the presence of sin, his love takes the form of mercy, and this says everything. Yes, everything. On one condition—that a sinner has to hope. And in a certain sense nobody has as much right to hope in God as the sinner.

"Divine holiness doubtless has such a horror of sin that justice punishes it in a frightfully painful manner. But that is precisely why divine mercy affects us incomparably more than all the misfortunes that could befall us. If, in fact, we look at it from the point of view of the punishment that sin deserves, it is the loss of God. Sin is therefore a supreme evil and truly absolute misery. But where will the greatest compassion go if not to the greatest misery? This is why divine mercy is more active here—so that the sinner repents, has confidence, obtains his pardon, and saves himself. Hence you see that even the ardor of God's anger is a new and more active source of pity and of goodness, and becomes for all of us a new basis for hope."[163]

Deeds of love

We have proved very clearly that mercy is nothing other than goodness. That is to say, mercy is the essence of God in relation to the misery of his creature. Should we not foresee that each of our faults can become a new occasion for this divine attribute to manifest and glorify itself?

Beati misericordes! With this beatitude, according to Monsignor Pie, one can say that the Son of God, made Man, revealed to us his own bliss and that of his Father in Heaven. The mercy that can be practiced by a simple mortal is for that person the beginning and a source of happiness. What then can we say of the mercy known and exercised by God alone! And what happiness will it continuously cause within the bosom of his divinity! *Blessed the merciful.* Therefore blessed is he above all others who alone has the right to be called *good. Unus est bonus Deus—One there is who is good* (Mt 19: 17). He whose essence is charity, he whose mercy and goodness have no other limit but infinity itself: *Confitemini Domino quoniam bonus, quoniam in aeternum misericordia eius—Give thanks to the Lord for he is good, for his steadfast love endures for ever* (Ps 136: 1). Lassitude has no place in God's nature. When God gives in to anger and imparts justice, he is faced with a task alien to his nature; *irascetur ut faciat . . . alienum opus eius—he will be wroth to do his deed . . . strange is his deed* (Is 28: 21). It is the left hand that holds the rod, and God tires very quickly when he uses this hand, *peregrinum opus eius ab eo—alien is his work* (ibid.). The right hand, however, is the favorite instrument of his heart. It performs deeds of love. In a fraction of a second it transforms a blind and incorrigible sinner into a resolute penitent: *haec mutatio dexterae Excelsi—the right hand of the Most High has changed* (Ps 77: 10).[164]

Furthermore, mercy can be imparted only if there is misery. What misery can be worse than sin! What can be a more pitiable object for infinite pity! The weight of these faults crushes us and makes us victims of divine wrath. It is up to us to give them value in God's sight. This should become a unique opportunity for God to show an attribute that seems dearer to him than justice; namely, goodness and love. It is up to us to appeal to his heart and to tell him with David, *Pardon me Lord, you will remove my faults,* to glorify your most dear perfection—mercy; *for your goodness' sake.* You will glorify it in proportion as you wipe out my numerous crimes and the multitude of my failings. All this gives me greater hope for forgiveness: *propitiaberis peccato meo, multum est enim—For thy name's sake, O Lord, pardon my guilt, for it is great* (Ps 24: 7, 11).

A well-known writer[165] adds: "God is the master who teaches us not to let evil anger us but to conquer evil with goodness; not to return evil for evil, nor to curse when cursed (1 Pet 3: 9), but heap goodness on our enemies and in this way load their heads with the burning coals of ardor (Rom 12: 20). *A disciple is not above his teacher, nor a servant above his master* (Mt 10: 24). Here we see the disciples of the divine master practicing this lesson to perfection. In this way they not only showed themselves full of benevolence and gentleness toward their sinful persecutors and cruel tyrants, but they returned them good for evil. They did this to the extent of sacrificing their lives to save them. What then should we say of the master who taught these just persons to practice such a sublime doctrine?

"When compared to the charity of Christ, the charity of all the disciples put together does not equal even a drop of water in the ocean. If, then, a spark of charity has been so effectively powerful in their case, what will a huge fire, as infinite as the supreme charity of God, not bring about?"

"Ah!" exclaimed St. John Chrysostom. "Jesus said to us: *If you love those who love you, what reward have you? . . . Do not even the Gentiles do the same?* (Mt 5:46–47). And we will say with God: If he hears and helps only the just, would his friends not miss part of his kindness?"

The sin, not the sinner

The infinite holiness of God, joined to his goodness, encourages him to pursue sin with hatred and the sinner with his mercy. Father Segneri says: "God holds sin in such great horror that to uproot it from our hearts not only did he humiliate himself, being clothed in mortal flesh unto death, but even today, glorious in the heavens, he humiliates himself to the extent of making himself a beggar: *Laboravi rogans* (Jer 15:6). But do you know why? Have you never observed a hunter at the moment he aims at his prey? See how he avoids the least noise, how he bends and, if necessary, creeps along the ground. Why? It is because he wants to kill the game that he aims at. Well, that is the aim of the prayers of our Lord, of his patience, and of his calm, of his silence while we offend him. He has only one aim: to exterminate sin and to exterminate it completely.

"If the Lord were to dispatch every guilty soul to hell, doubtless he would have killed every sinner, but he would not have exterminated sin. On the contrary, sin would become eternal when punished like this. Now, it is precisely because divine hatred attacks the fault directly and the sinner only indirectly that God goes to so much effort to separate the sinner from the sin, to wipe out sin while saving the sinner. He decides to let go of the guilty person only when he becomes stubborn of his own free will and no longer permits God to kill his sin. God is then forced to kill the sinner and the sin.

"Such an objective spurs on infinite Goodness to wait for us, to invite us to penance, and to welcome us. That is why David, knowing so well this disposition of God, and availing of it in a singular way, cried out: *O Lord, pardon my guilt, for it is great* (Ps 24: 11). A spirit unaware of divine workings would believe that the prophet was mistaken, and that he should have used the word 'great' to signify divine mercy and not his fault. His fault would then be excused and diminished. He could, then, with all sorts of considerations, demand its remission more boldly and obtain it more easily. But David was better advised. He knew that the enormity of sin is a reason for divine goodness. In order to exterminate it with greater satisfaction, he appealed to this very goodness saying to it: *Great is my sin*. He did this to purify his soul entirely. It is like the owner of a vineyard who, seeing it ravaged by a boar, describes the ferocity and the force of the animal in such exaggerated terms that the hunter is goaded into pursuing and killing it." [166]

Great is my sin

If David had previously used this language for the *God of armies*, with what confidence we can appeal to the Incarnate Word for the salvation of sinners—to him who wanted to assume our nature *ut misericors fieret*, precisely to make his mercy blossom more and become all-embracing. Bossuet does not hesitate to say: "Jesus Christ, as Son of God, is essentially holiness itself. Although he is pleased to see a sinner at his feet, returning to the true path, he would have preferred a strong innocent love that hadn't faltered. But, on becoming our Savior, his love for us took on a different sentiment. As God, he prefers innocence. But Christians, let us rejoice! For as a merciful Savior he has come in search of the guilty. He lives only for sinners because it is for sinners that he has been sent."[167] "His vocation is to be the Savior,"[168] repeats St. Francis de Sales. "He is the God of those who are miserable," continues the Venerable Mother Chappuis. "Each time we offer him a fault to be forgiven, we offer him the title of Savior."[169]

God forbid us from making any exaggerated or paradoxical statement. One is unwittingly reminded of what a great bishop told some missionaries who, in his presence, bemoaned the sins to which their ministry had made them witnesses. "Oh! what would be the very purpose of your existence, my good Fathers, if there had never been any sins?" What would you do here on earth with all the sacraments in the Church, if there had never been sins to forgive? Of what use is your mercy if there were no miserable persons to avail of it?

Jesus told St. Gertrude not to seek souls who are pure as brides to come to him. He said that he preferred they be sick and approach him as a doctor. A patient gives joy and honor to a doctor by placing full trust in his healing powers. In a similar way the sinner gives joy to the divine Samaritan, whom he asks to forgive his sins. If God is offended by sin, then the Savior is glorified by the forgiveness that destroys it. He would seem to want to flood the prodigal sinner with his gifts. In this way he has been offered a chance to satisfy his need and desire to forgive, for which we are grateful.

"Go then, my soul!" concludes St. Francis.[170] "As soon

as you feel ill, please do not hesitate to go immediately to the Doctor. Go with as great a confidence as possible. For, it is indeed for your sake that *he leaped out of his nuptial bed and with giant steps walked from the heights of Heaven* (see Ps 19: 5). He came to free you from the sickness of sin because he knew that it is the sick and not the healthy who need the doctor (see Mt 9: 12). How foolish are the sinners who seek an excuse to flee from the doctor, reasons that rather should inspire them with greater confidence to go to him. How stupid is he who takes for an adversary the man who has come to heal him!

"*The wicked flee when no one pursues* (Prov 28: 1). It is strange to flee without being pursued; but it is stranger still when an impious person flees with no one in pursuit. He flees even when divine goodness is calling after him, and running after him with mercy and a remedy for his ills, with the promise of all he needs for his salvation."

The Sacred Heart loves

The apparitions and the revelations of Paray-le-Monial illuminate this thinking with a gentle and delightful light! A saintly monk has very aptly said: "After the coming of our Lord, confidence should be the virtue of poor sinners." [171] But since the manifestation of the Sacred Heart of Jesus to the world, this confidence can be raised to daring heights. Did this Sacred Heart, after being pierced with the spear of Longinus, not pour over him forgiveness, but also sanctity and the grace of martyrdom? Is it not the heart that nourishes sinners with the blood that they have caused to flow, *like the pelican who feeds its little ones from its own breast which they have torn open.*[172] He wanted to be injured and opened up, as St. Vincent Ferrier has said, only to show to the guilty the very source of pardon. Is not this the infinite heart that cries to all from the depths of the tabernacle: *Come to me, all who labor and are heavy laden, and I will give you rest* (Mt 11:28)? Was he not devoured by an inexhaustible thirst to absolve and to cure, and do we not quench his thirst by bringing him our faults to be pardoned?

It should also be remarked that the souls who were very well initiated in the gentle secrets of the Sacred Heart were those who became, after sinning, the most zealous apostles and confident in the art of making use of our faults. The life of St. Gertrude demonstrates wonderful features of this kind, and St. Margaret Mary returns to it often. "The heart of Jesus," she said, "is the throne of mercy, where the most miserable are the best received, provided they possess love in the depths of their misery.

"When you have made mistakes, do not trouble yourself, because trouble and anxiety and too much impatience distance us from God and banish Jesus Christ from our hearts. But in asking him for pardon, let us pray to his Sacred Heart to make satisfaction to restore us to grace with his divine majesty. In complete confidence, then, say to the most lovable heart of Jesus: 'O my only love, pay for your poor slave and repair the harm that I have just done. Make me return to your glory; make me an example for my neighbor, and grant salvation to my soul.' In this manner, our failings sometimes serve to humiliate us and to make us realize what we are, and to what extent it is useful for us to be hidden in the depths of our nothingness.

"After humbling yourself, begin again to be faithful, because the Sacred Heart loves this way of acting which preserves the soul in peace." [173]

The venerated Father de la Colombière never ceased preaching on this topic. The following passage is taken from one of his letters to a soul crushed under the weight of its faults. One could hardly find a more faithful echo and a more practical summary of some of the teachings that St. Francis de Sales gives us.

"If I were in your place, this is how I would console myself. I would say to my God with confidence: 'Lord, here is a soul who is in the world to benefit from your admirable mercy, and to make it shine before heaven and earth. Others glorify you by the force of your grace, by their faithfulness and constancy. How gentle and generous you are toward those who are faithful to you! I, however, glorify you in making your goodness known to sinners. Mercy is above all malice. Nothing can exhaust it. No mistake, no matter how shameful or criminal it be, even if repeated again and again, should make a sinner despair of pardon. I have offended you gravely, O My lovable Redeemer! But it would be worse if I committed the horrible outrage of thinking that you are not good enough to pardon me. It is in vain that your enemy and mine sets new traps for me all the time. He can make me lose everything except my hope in your mercy. Had I fallen a hundred times, and my crimes were a hundred times more horrible than they are, I would still hope in you.'

"It seems to me that nothing that I could do to make reparation for my fault or the scandal that it would cause, would pain me. Then I would begin to serve God with greater fervor than before, and with the same tranquillity as if I had never offended him." [174]

The Venerable Mother Mary de Sales Chappuis, quoted earlier, occupied herself "in sounding the depths of the heart of God," as she herself put it. She was not at all afraid to say: "When, with every breath we fall and we give ourselves to God as often as we do, and begin again anew, the faults do not harm us. The Lord looks less at the faults than at the advantages we draw from them, provided we use them to humble ourselves before him and make ourselves small and gentle. They then do not harm us at all, nor do they weaken his good will toward us. It is a great grace for a soul to admit its fault. This knowledge helps it to discover the goodness of God and the worth of the divine Savior's merits."

7

Confidence in God's Mercy

(ii)

Being ashamed is a good start

We have seen how both theology and the saints say that our imperfections should lead to an increase in our trust in God's mercy.

Now let us hear our Saint himself: "You ask me, my dear daughters, if a soul full of its own misery can turn to God with full confidence? My answer is that the soul, aware of its misery, can have great confidence in God. In addition, this knowledge alone can inspire real confidence, and the recognition and confession of misery permits us to enter God's presence. Thus all the great saints, Job, David, and the others, began all their prayers by confessing their misery and their unworthiness. It is a good thing, then, to recognize oneself as being poor, base, abject, and unworthy to appear in God's presence.

"The famous saying of the ancients, 'know thyself,' refers primarily to the knowledge and excellence of the soul: in this way it is not degraded and desecrated by things unworthy of its nobility. But it also means understanding and knowing our unworthiness and misery. Thus, inasmuch as we know ourselves to be miserable, the more we will place our trust in the goodness and mercy of God. Between misery and mercy there is such a great link that the one cannot exist without the other. If

God had not created man, he would still have remained truly good; but then he could never have been merciful, because mercy is shown to those who are miserable.

"You see that the more we recognize ourselves as being miserable, the more opportunities we have to trust God, for we have nothing within us with which to trust ourselves. The mistrust of ourselves comes from the knowledge of our imperfections. It is good not to trust ourselves; but what good would it do us if we did not put our confidence in God and hope for his mercy?

"The mistakes and the acts of unfaithfulness that we commit every day must bring us shame and confusion when we want to approach our Lord. We read that there are great souls, like St. Catherine of Siena and St. Teresa of Avila, who, when they made a mistake, had a strong sense of shame. It is quite right that having offended God, we withdraw a little through humility and feel ashamed; because if we have offended a friend we are ashamed to meet him. But one should not remain in this state; the virtues of humility, abjection, and shame are means by which we must proceed to unite our soul with God. It would not be a great thing to annihilate and divest ourselves (which happens when we are ashamed), if it were not to give ourselves to God. It is in this sense that St. Paul teaches us when he says: *Put off the old nature . . . and put on the new* (Col 3: 9–10). This little withdrawal is made only to advance move effectively toward God by an act of love and confidence. Here, then, is the conclusion of the first point. It is very good to be ashamed because we thereby know and feel our misery and imperfections. However, we must neither stop nor be discouraged; rather, we must elevate our heart to God in holy trust. The foundation of this trust should be in him and not in us. All the more so because we change, and he never does; he always remains good and merciful, whether we are weak and imperfect or whether we are strong and perfect.

"I am often saying that our misery is the throne of God's mercy. The greater our misery, the greater the trust that we must have." [175]

Christ's tenderness toward the weak

"You have no reason to doubt God's love for you. He looks with love on the worst sinners of the world, despite their lack of will to convert themselves. For his weak creatures he has a gentle, pleasant, condescending, and loving heart, provided they recognize their misery. He is so gracious toward those who are miserable, and so good to penitents. Who could not love this royal Heart, which is so paternal as well as maternal in affection toward us? . . .

"We should not take pleasure in our imperfections; but with the great Apostle we must say: *Wretched man that I am! Who will deliver me from this body of death?* (Rom 7:24). But these imperfections must not astonish us, nor discourage us. We should draw from them the virtues of submission, humility, and mistrust of ourselves, but not discouragement or affliction of the heart, much less doubt the love of God for us. God does not love our imperfections and venial sins, but he loves us despite them. A mother's love does not decrease because of the infirmity and weakness of a child; she still loves the child tenderly and with compassion. In the same way, God does not love imperfections or venial sins, but he does not stop loving us tenderly. David was right to say to our Lord: *Be gracious to me, O Lord, for I am languishing* (Ps 6:2).

"My dear daughter, live joyously. Our Lord looks at you, and he watches over you affectionately. His tenderness for you is proportionate to your great weakness.

Never cherish contrary ideas in your mind. When they assail you, do not pay attention to them; turn away your eyes from your weakness, and turn them toward God courageously and with humility. Speak to him of his ineffable kindness by which he loves our feeble, poor, and abject human nature, despite its miseries." [176]

"Take pride in being nothing. Be at ease, for God can be merciful because your misery is the object of his goodness.

"The most miserable beggars and those whose wounds are the most terrible are considered the best and the most suitable to receive charity. We can only be in the beggars' position. God's mercy watches over them willingly and protects them.

"Let us be humble, I beg you, and show only our wounds and miseries at the door of the temple of divine pity. But while taking consolation in having nothing, remember to show them joyfully, so that our Lord fills you with his kingdom." [177]

"The strongest argument of beggars is to expose their ulcers and their needs to us." [178]

"You ask me regarding the absolution of your sins of so many years. My dearest daughter, you must know that God in his goodness would have removed them at the very moment you wanted to give him your heart. He would have done this when through his inspiration you decided to live only for him. However, my dearest sister, you would do well to repeat the prayer of the penitent who said: *Lord, wash me thoroughly from my iniquity, and cleanse me from my sin* (Ps 51:2). This should be done with a true and simple trust in his sovereign goodness with the certainty that his mercy will not let you down." [179]

"Raise up your heart often toward our Redeemer with a

holy confidence, with deep humility, and say: I am miserable, Lord; put my misery into your merciful bosom and lead me with your fatherly hand to the enjoyment of your heritage. I am feeble and miserable, but you will welcome me on the day of my death, because I have hoped in you and I have desired to belong to you." [180]

"I swear to you on our common love which is Jesus Christ, that despite your misery you will live in peace. *I will all the more gladly boast of my weaknesses, so that the power of Christ may rest upon me* (2 Cor 12:9), our great St. Paul has said. Our misery is the throne where the sovereign goodness of our Lord is made known." [181]

"May your misery and your act of humility, pure and sincere, be used to praise God on the throne of his goodness." [182]

"My dear daughter, remain in peace; never be disturbed by your imperfections. Rather raise your eyes high toward the infinite goodness of him who, in order to keep us in humility, permits us to live with our infirmities. Put all your confidence in his goodness, and he will take care of your soul and everything concerning it, better than you could ever think of doing yourself.

"If you have not lived up to these expectations until now, there is a remedy. Henceforth you should conform to this teaching. Your miseries and your infirmities should not surprise you. God has seen many more. His mercy does not reject those who are miserable but desires to do good to them, and to use their misery for his glory." [183]

"Certainly our miseries and our weaknesses, however grievous they may be, must not discourage us; they must, rather, make us humble and lead us to throw ourselves into the arms of divine mercy. This mercy will be glorified in us in proportion to our miseries, provided we rise out of them. We should hope to be able to do this with the grace of our Lord." [184]

Advice to confessors and spiritual directors

St. Francis de Sales wanted people responsible for the behavior of others to be especially careful, so as to give them courage and strengthen their trust. For this reason, he wrote to a superior who had become notorious, sadly, because of a young girl whom he had recommended to her care.[185] "But you see, you are a little too severe toward this poor girl. You must not reprimand her so much, because she is full of good will. Tell her, even if she makes a lot of mistakes, that she should never be too surprised at this. Let her rather gaze at our Lord, who, from heaven above, looks on her as a father at his child who is still too weak to walk firmly, and says: 'Slowly, my child.' If she falls, he encourages her, saying: 'What a lovely leap! How clever!' Then he goes close to her and holds her hand. If this daughter is humble, and if she knows that she is a child, she will never be surprised at her fall; then she will never fall from a great height." [186]

The saintly Doctor gave similar and even more specific instructions for confessors. Having reminded them that penitents address them in the name of the Father, he advises that they should have "a fatherly heart for them, receiving them with extreme love, despite their defects." He adds: "Thus, even though the prodigal child returns completely naked, dirty, and smelling because of the swine, this good father nevertheless embraces him with love, and weeps over him. He does this because he is a father, and the hearts of fathers are tender for their children."

The Saint also shows how one should welcome a beaten and despairing penitent: "If you see him afraid and broken down, and he is doubtful of obtaining pardon for his sins, raise him up while pointing out to him the great pleasure that God gets from the repentance of terrible sinners. The worse our misery, the greater the glory it will bring God's mercy. Show him that our Lord prayed to God his Father for those who crucified him to make us understand that, when we crucified him with our own hands, he pardoned us with great generosity. God has such a great regard for true repentance that the least conversion in the world makes him forget all sorts of sins. This, to such an extent, that even if the dammed and the devils could have it, all their sins would be forgiven. The greatest saints were notorious sinners: St. Peter, St. Matthew, St. Mary Magdalen, David, and so on. In fact, the worst wrong that we can do to God, as well as to the Passion and death of Jesus Christ, is not to hope to obtain pardon for our sins. Through faith, we are obliged to believe in the remission of sins, so that we do not doubt at all the sacrament that we receive, which our Lord has instituted to this effect." [187]

Love-sorrow for each fault

We know with what perfection the gentle Francis de Sales practiced this kindness with regard to his penitents. Such sentiments filled him, and he used them himself. His contemporaries and those whom he trusted tell us: "I have often heard the interest that St. Teresa of Avila had for reading the lives of saints who had been sinners. This preference can be explained, for thereby she was able to see the magnificence of divine mercy shining above their great misery." [188]

"I don't know how I am made," wrote St. Francis to St. Jeanne de Chantal. "I feel miserable, but I don't trouble myself about it; and sometimes I am even happy in thinking that I am a really good object for the mercy of God."

Finally, Father La Rivière speaks of the saintly bishop's saying that it is not possible to express the love-sorrow he felt for each fault: a pain blended always with filial fear, a bitter-sweet emotion of absolute abandon and complete hope in God's incomprehensible goodness. "No, it certainly is not possible to express that, since this excellent person, from his tender youth, had been instructed by the Holy Spirit to see God as extremely good and lovable, even in the midst of his own imperfections. These last are totally destroyed by God when we repent for them. He wipes them out in the ocean of his mercy and consumes them in the fire of his infinite charity. With this in mind, if one sometimes becomes slightly weak and does not live up to one's good resolutions, then he, without getting angry or impatient, should start again gently and look toward the benign Savior with perfect confidence."[189]

8

Strengthening Our Perseverance

A state of alertness

The subject of this chapter has been implicitly dealt with in preceding pages. In fact, it is simply the conclusion to the last two chapters. Our failings obtain for us a more exact knowledge of our weaknesses. In giving us a greater right in some way to obtaining God's mercy, these failings should naturally incline us to be more on our guard, and to return with a more trustful humility to God, without whom we can do nothing, and with whom we can achieve everything. It is well known that, in spiritual combat, distrust of oneself and confidence in God are sure signs of victory.

In God's design, moreover, our faults are called upon to render to our perseverance services that are important from several points of view. First of all, it is clear that they must make us more vigilant. This is one of the meanings that the interpreters give to the sacred text: *Infirmitas gravis sobriam facit animam*—a serious illness makes the soul temperate (Sir 31:2).

"Without doubt," says St. John Chrysostom, "it should suffice us to see that men superior to us in holiness were not spared from making mistakes; this encourages us to be more circumspect and to practice greater prudence."[190] "Our personal mistakes are our most successful teachers. Our nature is such that it needs to stumble against rocks in order to verify this painful reality." [191]

The Holy Spirit, as well as experience, demonstrates this truth. *He that is inexperienced knows few things* (Sir 34: 10). A Father of the Church, commenting on this text, says: "A serene happiness is dangerous. The fear of falling into a trap again makes a person more careful—just as a navigator who has known danger is more on his guard, and the memory of a single shipwreck, caused by his imprudence, makes him ever wary of inhospitable ports." [192]

This alertness is the first lesson that we should draw from our mistakes. We should recognize and fight against their causes and avoid the lack of foresight and superficiality. Above all, we should flee willful occasions: the demon of demons, as they have been called, that devours so many souls. Sailors have their charts whereon they carefully mark the reefs they have seen. In the light of our experience with previous faults, let us also chart out our own map for spiritual navigation. These maps will describe the causes of our previous desertions, our inclinations and vain illusions, the precautions not taken, and the times when we have been led astray. Wiser, as a result of our sad experiences, we will henceforth avoid the rocks revealed to us by our shipwrecks.

Sentinels on guard

St. Francis de Sales does not fail to offer us advice: "In your letters I have seen your little failings and imperfections, at which neither you nor I should be surprised. These are small warnings for us to keep low and humble in our own eyes, and like sentinels to remain on guard over ourselves." [193]

"Spiritual fevers, like bodily ones, are generally followed by several types of irritation. They are useful for the one who is cured, for several reasons; the principal one is that they consume the residual ill-humor caused by the sickness. This process happens in such a way that not a trace remains. They also refresh our memory of some former illness and make us afraid of falling again. Often we are prone to falling by too much licence and liberty, and we would be overtaken again were we not restrained by earlier experiences and be on our guard until we were assured of good health." [194]

"In order not to become worse, we must never forget what we were in the past." [195]

Faithful to the means for perseverance

From this first benefit drawn from our mistakes, a second naturally follows: namely, remaining faithful to those means that help us persevere. Each one of our failings will then become an irresistible preacher on the need for grace and the duty to receive it through prayer and frequent reception of the sacraments. These humiliations serve to shake us out of our lethargy and to stimulate our ardor for the service of God and the pursuit of virtue. According to Father Pinamonti, "There is no faster steed than the horse that has escaped the wolf's claws. It feels this enemy at his flanks all the time. It does not run—it flies. Such is the effect produced in the saints by their failures. It spurs them on to do more good." [196]

St. John Chrysostom noticed these happy results in his friend Theodore. He wrote: "When a hunter just grazes a lion, he makes it more furious and invincible. In the same way, the enemy of the human race, in trying to inflict a deep wound on you, redoubles your generosity and your devotion to good works." [197]

St. Epiphanius expressed the same idea in a charming analogy. "When a stag feels old age approaching, he lies in wait at the side of the rocks near a snake's nest. He puts his mouth to the opening; then he sucks and swallows the reptile. Immediately, with the effort strengthened by the presence of a poisonous morsel and driven by a devouring thirst, he launches out in search of pure water. If he finds it within three hours, he drinks for himself fifty new years of life. In the same way, O spiritual man, if the serpent of sin penetrates your heart, fly to the sources of grace, and there through repentance, not only will your sin be effaced, but your strength will be restored." [198]

According to Father Grou: "A child who wants to walk on his own, leaves his mother for a while, but then falls. He returns to her with greater tenderness to be healed of the injury he has caused himself. His fall has taught him not to leave his mother again. The experience of his weakness and the kindness with which his mother receives him inspire him to be more attached to her." [199]

A holy fear and distrust in self

One finds the basis of all these thoughts in the writings of our most lovable Saint. "Take your heart and place it gently in the hands of our Lord, begging him to cure it. On your side, do all that you can by renewing your resolutions: through reading books and other appropriate means suitable to cure you. If you do this, you will gain much from your loss and live a more healthy life through the experience of your illness." [200]

"Self-love, self-esteem, false liberty of the mind, cannot be easily eradicated from the human heart. But we can prevent sins, which are their fruits, from being committed. As long as we are in this mortal life, we cannot absolutely prevent their thrusts, their blows, their new shots—that is to say, their first offensive. We can, however, moderate them and diminish their frequency and ardor by the practice of the contrary virtues, and especially the love of God. We need to be patient and gradually to correct and cut out our bad habits, tame our aversions, and overcome our inclinations and ill-humor as they arise. On the whole, my dear daughter, this life is a continual war, and there isn't anybody who can say: I was never attacked. Rest is reserved for heaven, where the palm branch of victory awaits us. On earth we should always fight as though we are between fear and hope. But we must do so, knowing that hope will always be the stronger, bearing in mind the power of the One who comes to our aid."[201]

"My God, how joyful is the inner kingdom, when this saintly love reigns there! How blessed are the powers of our soul that obey so saintly and wise a king! No, my dear cousin, under his obedience and in this state, he doesn't allow great sins to dwell there, or any attachment toward the smallest of them. It is true that he allows them to approach the frontier, so as to exercise the inner virtues in the war and make them more valiant. He permits spies—that is to say, our venial sins, our imperfections—to run here and there in his kingdom; but that is only to make known that without him we would fall prey to all our enemies."[202]

"What do you want me to say, my dear daughter, on your relapse into misery, if not that it is a return to the enemy? It is necessary to take up arms again and pluck up the courage to fight harder than ever. . . . But, my God! guard against falling into any kind of discouragement. Heavenly kindness will not allow these failings to be the occasion for abandoning you, but to humiliate you and draw you closer and more firmly into the hands of his mercy."[203]

"You see, my dear sister, it often happens that thinking we are entirely free of these old enemies whom we have overcome, we find them approaching from a direction we least expected. Solomon, that singular wise man of the world, worked so many wonders in his youth. But he became overconfident, with his great virtues and his past. When he seemed to be out of danger from attack, he was surprised by the enemy whose appearance he least feared.

"From this we can learn two lessons: One, that we must always distrust ourselves and walk in holy fear, continually asking heaven for help, and live a simple devout life. The other, that our enemies may be pushed back, but they are not killed. They sometimes leave us in peace; but this is only a lull before the storm.

"But, my dearest sister, you must not be discouraged by this at all. The small shocks make us look deeper into ourselves, to accept our weakness, and then to run back more quickly to our protector. St. Peter walked on the waves with a little too much self-assurance. The wind rose, and the waves seemed to swallow him. Then he cried out: 'Lord, save me!' And our Lord, taking him by the arm said to him: 'O man of little faith, why did you doubt?' It is in the midst of our troubles and our passions, in the winds and storms of temptations, that we call out to the Savior. He permits us to be troubled only to provoke us into invoking him more ardently." [204]

Seeking God's help always

"Let us be humble. Let us admit that if it were not for God's being a sword and shield for us, we would be immediately pierced through and through by all kinds of sins. Let us therefore remain close to God through spiritual exercises. Let this be our primary business, and all the rest secondary." [205]

"If sometimes self-love and weakness shake you up, never be disturbed; for God allows it in order to be able to shake hands with you, so that you humble yourself and demand his paternal help." [206]

"When we feel it difficult to keep away from sin, or when we are afraid of being unable to resist these occasions or temptations, we should not doubt whether we have the required amount of trust in God. No! Because mistrust of our strength is not a sign of lack of resolution but a true recognition of our misery.

"To doubt our power of resisting temptations is a healthier approach than the overconfident one, provided that we do not expect too much from our own forces but depend on the grace of God. Many souls, having received too much consolation, have promised to perform miracles for God. But when the moment for action came, they failed. On the other hand, several who did not have great confidence in their strength and were afraid that they would not be able to live up to their expectations performed miracles. This great feeling that they were weak pushed them to seek God's help—to watch, pray, and be humble so as not to fall into temptation.

"It could happen that we feel within us neither the strength nor the courage to resist when faced with temptation. Nevertheless, God will help us on condition that we want to resist it, and that we hope for his help. When we ask for his help, we will never be disappointed. All the more so because there is no need to have always within us the feeling of strength and courage. It is enough to hope to have it at the opportune moment. So there is no need to fear any sign of discouragement within oneself. It is enough to put our hope in God's help. It was only when he needed it that Samson felt the supernatural strength given by God. It is said that when he came across lions and enemies, God's spirit took hold of him in order to kill them. And God, who does nothing in vain, does not give us the strength or the courage if it is not needed. However, he never fails on these occasions. We must always make use of David's words: *Why are you cast down, O my soul, and why are you disquieted within me? Hope in God* (Ps 43:5); and of this prayer which he used: *Do not cast me off in the time of old age; forsake me not when my strength is spent* (Ps 71:9)." [207]

"Humility is the big secret for maintaining proper devotion. Be humble, and God will be with you; your good will shall increase, and you shall give yourself to him without disguise and reserve, asking him from the bottom of your heart that, if you have not served him well until now, he in his goodness might forgive you. Ask him, too, to strengthen your resolution to detach yourself from all the attachments of the world and attach yourself only to the love of God and serve him faithfully and whole-heartedly. . . . We should not trouble ourselves concerning our offenses, for the divine Spirit is often more liberal in his gifts to those who were the most niggardly toward him in their hearts and affections." [208]

"I hope our Lord will always hold out his hand to you, and that you will never trip. If you stumble against a stone and fall, it will only help you to be better on your guard, and to make you cry out more for the help of this gentle heavenly Father. I pray to him to keep you always under his holy protection. Amen." [209]

"Even if we were to be the most perfect persons in the world, we should never know to recognize it, but consider ourselves always imperfect. Our examination must never lead us to question whether we are imperfect—for that we must never doubt. It follows that we must never be astonished at finding ourselves imperfect, since we should never see ourselves any different in this life. We should not be saddened by it, because there is no cure for it. On the other hand, in humbling ourselves we make reparation for our defects, and change slowly. Indeed, our imperfections have been left with us for this exercise. Hence, we could not be excused if we did not try to change, although we will continue to have defects—we won't manage to change completely—because it is not as easy to avoid imperfections as it is to avoid sins." [210]

Unpleasant memories

Finally, the last advantage to be drawn from our faults. It lies in recalling the remorse they have left in us, the torments they have caused us, and the reparation that we have been required to carry out. Let us make use of our disgust at having to submit ourselves to these unpleasant details, so that we keep ourselves from falling again. Let us tell ourselves at the time of temptation: "My soul, remember the troubles created by these faults, when you had the misfortune of previously committing them." Remind yourself what it has cost you to abandon them, to efface their trace, and to make reparation for the consequences. Remember the anguish and torture caused by the weight of your sins, the terrors that crushed you then at the thought of the judgment of God, as well as the shame you had to overcome before admitting them at the holy tribunal. Remind yourself of all this and spare yourself the trouble of experiencing these pains, torments, and humiliations, by being more generous and faithful.

Doubtless such motives are far from being perfect, but rather have more to do with fear than with love. Nevertheless, they can still be put to profit and deserve to be mentioned among the efforts listed in the "art" of profiting from our faults. Our good Saint hardly insists on this but does not omit it. "Love is courageous and is strong enough to sustain itself because of the place where it finds itself; namely, the human heart, which is ever changing and subject to rebellion. That is why love uses fear in combat and also to make the enemy retreat."[211]

9

How to Become More Fervent

Repentance

This chapter leads us to our final position on the art of profiting from our faults. It should also help us attain the height of all perfection: the ardor of divine love.

If some of our readers want to know more about the genesis of love through repentance, they may refer to the final chapters of the second book of the *Treatise on the Love of God*. Suffice it to recall here that this last-mentioned virtue—repentance—deals with our sins. So it should easily be understood how they benefit us.

Repentance is made up of various acts. Here it will be viewed in terms that, in theological and popular parlance, are known as *acts of the penitent*. Confession, contrition, and satisfaction are the substance, or at least the essence, of the sacrament of reconciliation.

Our dear Doctor gives us a sublime teaching on each of these three points. In the light of his words, we will discover the treasures our faults bring us. They do so by nourishing those acts our souls perform in repenting. Self-accusation seems to be the first. It includes the ceaseless effort of attracting blessings, as a powerful means of converting our faults into merit.

"The loving heart of our Redeemer measures and organises all events in the world. He does all this for the benefit of souls who want to respond wholeheartedly to his divine love. . . . It is there, my dear, that our faults are thorns in our souls. But once removed through voluntary self-accusation, they are subsequently transformed into roses and perfumes. They enter our heart through our malice, but they are thrown out by the Holy Spirit."[212]

"The scorpion's sting is poisonous the moment it bites; but the oil drawn from it is an effective remedy against its own sting. Sin is shameful when we commit it; but once converted through confession and repentance, it becomes honorable and salutary.

"Contrition and confession are so beautiful and so fragrant that they wipe away the ugliness of sin and purify its stench. Simon the leper called Mary Magdalen a sinner, but our Lord did not agree with him. He spoke only of the perfumes she poured out and of her great charity. If we are truly humble, Philothea, our sins will be infinitely offensive to us, for God is offended by them. But a declaration of our sins will be pleasant and agreeable because God is honored by it. Just telling the doctor of the pain that torments us gives us some kind of relief. When you kneel before your spiritual director, imagine yourself to be on Mount Calvary, at the feet of Jesus Christ crucified. His precious blood seeps through each of your pores to wash away your sins. Although it is not the physical blood of the Savior, what flows so abundantly over penitents in confessionals is the merit of his Blood. Open wide your heart, then, so that you can cast out your sins in confession. As fast as they leave, the precious merits of Christ's Passion will enter there and fill it with blessings."[213]

In confession, "you will also practice the virtues of humility, obedience, simplicity, and charity. You will exercise more virtues in this single act of confession than in any other act whatsoever."[214]

"If sin has made man guilty, then confession and contrition make him infinitely more honorable." [215]

"O Lord! What happiness the heart of a loving father experiences when he hears his daughter confess that she was envious and cunning! This envy is a blessing indeed, for it is followed by such a frank confession! By writing your letter, your hand made a more courageous gesture than any made by Alexander." [216]

Father du Pont has some striking comments on this subject. He outlines the multiplicity of virtuous acts practiced in confessing our faults. He doesn't hesitate to consider it a superhuman degree of virtue. According to him, this is what Job seems to suggest, for he bears witness to God as never having *concealed my transgressions from men, by hiding my iniquity in my bosom* (Job 31:33).

St. Gregory states that it often requires more courage to confess a sin than it takes to avoid it. We know the words of St. Augustine: "God accepts your faults. But if you accept them yourself, you find yourself united to him."

When one realizes that a sin committed once can become, with repeated self-accusation, an occasion for unassailable virtues and merits, don't we have the right to repeat: *Felix culpa!* (*O happy fault!*)?

The sacred fire of his love

The same thoughts apply, more forcefully, to contrition. It is here that the author of *Theotimus* reveals the role of divine charity "with its loving anguish and its anguished love."

As far as I know, nature does not convert fire into water. Water, however, has been converted to fire. God once worked this miracle. It is written in the Book of Maccabees (2 Mac 1:19) that when the children of Israel were led to Babylon, at the time of Sedecras, the priests, on the advice of Jeremiah, hid the sacred fire in the hollow of a dry well. On their return, the children of those who had hidden the fire went in search of it as instructed by their fathers. They found it had changed into very viscous liquid. On the orders of Nehemiah, they took it and sprinkled it on the sacrifices. As soon as the rays of the sun shone, it was transformed again into a huge fire.

"Theotimus, in the midst of trials and the lament of true repentance, God very often places the sacred fire of his love in our heart itself. This is transformed into the water of copious tears. Through a second transformation it becomes a huge fire of love again. Similarly, the famous repentant lover first of all loves the Savior, then transforms this love into tears, and these tears then turn to form a most excellent *eau-de-vie*. This is why our Lord says that many sins were forgiven because she had loved much. We see that fire changes wine into a liquid called the *water of life* in some places. This sets alight and so easily feeds a fire that it is called *ardent*—burning. In the same way, when Goodness, the object of our loving consideration and lovable in itself, is offended by sin, the liquid of holy repentance is produced. And this, in turn, becomes the fire of divine love, which can indeed be called *eau-de-vie* (water of life) and *ardent*." [217]

The power of love

"I beg of you, Theotimus, to look at dear Magdalen, how she weeps with love: *They have taken away my Lord, and I don't know where they have laid him*. But after finding him through sighs and tears, she holds onto and possesses him through love. Imperfect love desires and needs him. Repentance seeks and finds him. Perfect love holds and embraces him. They say that in their natural state the rubies of Ethiopia have a very pale color of fire. But after being immersed in vinegar, they are set aflame and shine stunningly. So, too, love prior to repentance is normally imperfect, but immersed in the acidity of repentance it is reinforced and becomes excellent love." [218]

"It is not correct to equate the power of sin with the power of charity. For sin is the result of our weakness, and charity comes from the strength of God. If sin abounds in destructive malice, grace is overflowing. God's mercy, which wipes off sins, is exalted and gloriously triumphant against the severity of judgment (Jas 2:13). Thus our Lord through his miracles not only healed bodies, not only restored people to health, but also gave them blessings, making them victorious against illness: such was his goodness toward man." [219]

St. Bernard speaks of a perfume he calls *the ointment of contrition*. According to him, "it is an ointment that the soul, burdened by sins, makes up for herself. This she does while reflecting on her conduct. She gathers, heaps up, and crushes in the mortar of conscience the many and varied species of sins. And in the crucible of a fervent heart, she melts down and fuses all, together with repentance and sorrow, supplying the necessary heat. She can now say with the psalmist: *My heart became hot within me. As I mused, the fire burned* (Ps 38:3)". We need not go far in search of this perfume, for we find it without effort "within the little gardens of our consciences, and we can collect it whenever we need it. For, if we wish to be sincere, which of us has not always enough sins and iniquity ready to hand?" [220]

New merits

The strongest and most powerful feelings pressure the truly repentant soul. They enter it through the breach caused by sin. There they increase a hundredfold her love for the insulted divinity. The soul expresses sorrow for having hurt God's love, gratitude for his patience and gifts so generously and repeatedly given. She also asks him to forget her past unfaithfulness and to grant her something bitter and sweet at the same time, to make her weep along with Mary Magdalen in the presence of the Savior. We weep in the measure in which he allows us to kiss his feet and gives us a merciful welcome to our repentance. Isn't all this good enough reason to light up in the contrite soul a flame of charity unknown before the fault itself was committed? If we foster these dispositions when we recall our sins, what heavenly illuminations will be attained!

"The more you plunge into divine love, the more penetrating this memory becomes, and it stimulates the need to love the Being who has so shamefully been insulted," says Benigne Gojos.[221] The fault may have lasted for only an instant, but the fire of love lasts a lifetime. It can redouble each time we think of this fault. It can become eternal.

Certainly, every time we savor the recollection of a mistake we have willingly made, it is a further stain. But it is also true that each time a repentant soul condemns, regrets, and disowns its earlier sins, she receives the compensation of new merits. And because such repudiations can be multiplied infinitely, one can hardly imagine the sum of all these merits and what they could achieve!

According to an old tradition, there is not one pilgrim who, while passing in front of the tomb of Absalom in the valley of Josaphat, does not throw a stone at it or insult the memory of this cruel son. And yet, this tomb, buried under the pile of stones of public indignation, has become a monument that demonstrates the respect people have for the fourth commandment: *Honor your father and your mother.*

In the same way, if each of our faults is made the object of unceasing regret, it can serve as a base to build a mountain of merit.

When we confess our past sins, who knows the value of the fruitfulness that sacramental absolution adds to each repentance! Sanctifying grace flows once again in greater abundance, in proportion to the penitent's disposition. In addition, the blood of Jesus Christ, like divine crimson, covers over the marks left by the sins blotted out; it leaves the sap of supernatural strength there, often more vigorous than it was before the fall.

From this point of view, we can understand the apparently paradoxical sayings of those who have dealt with or talked about the *art of profiting from one's faults.* In the presence of a very fervent community, an enlightened nun once said: "My sisters, a fault is sometimes more profitable than receiving Holy Communion!" Yes, in a certain way, because, at times, the correction and repentance for a fault produce a more lasting effect, or at least a more sensitive one, than the very reception of the Author of Grace in Holy Communion.

In all these reflections there is an infinite ocean of consolation. One feels obliged to apply to sin what the prophet Hosea and the Apostle St. Paul say of death: *Death is swallowed up in victory*, in the victory of love.[222]

The Practice of Making Satisfaction

What does "making satisfaction" mean?

According to St. Gregory, love cannot remain inactive: "It manifests itself in deeds." And the recollection of our faults should be used to produce such deeds. The fervor it produces should not remain at the level of feelings. It should rule over our will and be reflected in our behavior. The sorrow of true repentance, says our beloved Saint, should not so much be called sorrow as displeasure or a detestation of evil. "It is a sorrow that is never irritating or despondent, and it by no means burdens the spirit, but makes it active, prompt, and diligent. It doesn't wound the heart but gives it an uplift through prayer and hope, and it is expressed in the fervor of devotion. . . . Further, it is attentive and full of affection, and its purpose is to resist, reject, and prevent past and future evils."[223] "Our imperfections are an important part of humility and lead to generosity and confidence."[224]

The duty of giving *satisfaction* is the principal lever of true penance. According to St. Anselm, satisfaction consists in giving God due honor. For St. Augustine, satisfaction is to uproot the causes of sin, and to give no opening to suggestions to sin. St. Thomas[225] explains these two different definitions and reconciles them in an admirable manner. But whatever be the definition, satisfaction will always indicate the path that our shortcomings should travel in order for us to benefit from them.

If we realize how much we have offended God by even the smallest of our sins, then we should also recall what fervor would be necessary to compensate for the offense caused to his Divine Majesty! Should not our faults move us to greater fidelity in proportion to their gravity and number? This outcome would be in keeping with the words of the prophet: *Turn to him in the measure of your having revolted* (see Is 31:6). Will not all the creatures who have schemed in our evil now use their voices to cry out at the sins that they made us commit? *Get behind me and do not touch me.* Or, at least do not make use of me in the future, unless it is to correct your criminal past! And should we not feel the need to double and triple the hours God still gives us in order to make up for lost time? From here on, let us be patient in bearing the excruciating consequences of our sins. By hard and pious work, through mortification, let us avenge within us the rights of God we have violated. From here on, with jealous impatience, we will devote all our faculties and every one of our moments to him.

Suffering the pain of sin

St. Francis de Sales recommends in one of his letters: "My daughter, go in peace, your confessions have been good even to excess. From now on, concentrate on progressing in virtue and think no longer of your past sins. If at all you do so, it should be to humble yourself before God, who has forgiven you by means of the Divine Sacrament, and beg for his mercy." [226]

"You know that your faults have delayed your progress in virtue. Well, then, humble yourself before God, implore his mercy, prostrate yourself before his goodness, and beg for his forgiveness. Confess your faults, and thank him through the ear of your confessor in order to receive absolution. Having done this, remain in peace. After detesting your mistake, lovingly accept the consequent displeasure at your slow spiritual progress. Alas! my Theotimus, souls in Purgatory are probably there because of their sins, which they detested supremely. However, as regards the regret and pain they suffer, they do so by being detained in a state deprived for a time of the joy of the blessed in Paradise. They suffer this state lovingly and sing with devotion the canticle of divine justice: *Righteous art thou, O Lord, and right are thy judgments* (Ps 119: 137)."

One would be quite justified in asking: Is it possible to accept God's will if an inspired work comes to nought because of the mistake of the one to whom it was entrusted? For, although it is permitted by God, this result is not of God's will but of my failing. "It is true, my child, that your fault is not produced by the will of God, for God is not the author of sin. However, the divine will permits your fault to bring about your undoing and your failure as a punishment. Although his goodness does not will your fault, his justice wants you to suffer from the consequent pain. He did not want David to sin, either. But he inflicted on him the pain of his sin. He is not the cause of Saul's sin, but allowed him to be defeated as a punishment.

"When the plans of God do not succeed in punishing our faults, on our part we should hate the mistake through sincere repentance and accept the pain that follows. Just as sin is against God's will, so also pain is the result of his permitting it." [227]

The fruits of reparation

St. Francis de Sales does not want us merely to accept the harmful consequences of our shortcomings simply as punishment. He wants us to correct them by redoubling our efforts. "But you might well ask what we should do to make up for lost time. You should live the remaining part of your lives more fervently and diligently." [228]

As a true disciple of her dear father, St. Jeanne de Chantal often repeated to her daughters these encouraging remarks: "You ask, 'How can we see the will of God in our faults and in our imperfections?' Yes, my dear children—we can always see his will, permitting us to fall into imperfections so as to make us humble. We accuse ourselves, we love our misery, and, in so doing, make reparation for our faults and obtain pardon for them." [229]

Such has been the practice of the saints: "They rise up from their fall," says St. Ambrose, "more ardent and more resolute to fight; so much so, that their faults, rather than being an obstacle, are an occasion to redouble their fervor." [230]

St. John Chrysostom adds: "Men who previously rushed impetuously into doing evil, now do good with the same fervor, all the more so as they cannot get rid of their huge debts: *He who is forgiven little loves little* (Lk 7:47)." Consumed by the fire of repentance, they make their souls purer than the purest gold. The strength of their conscience and the memory of past transgressions, like an impetuous wind, then blows full sail along the course of virtue. In this way, they are better than those who have never stumbled. Repentance, as the Scriptures have shown us, endows the converted sinner with a splendor greater than that of the just. That is why *the tax collectors and the harlots go into the kingdom of God before you* (Mt 21: 31). That is why *many that are first will be last, and the last first* (Mt 19: 30)." [231]

Lost innocence

But the following objection may also be raised. Would it appear that penitent sinners are better off than the just who have never erred, over those who have preserved their innocence intact? We have absolutely no intention of equating virtue kept intact with virtue reinstated. Innocence has a greater resemblance to the infinite sanctity of God. It is a close imitation of God. It is greatly loved by his Son, who has appropriated it for himself and his Mother. Never can the bitter perfumes of repentance equal the pure aroma that exudes from a pure life. Just as the lily stands out among other flowers, so also innocence always retains a striking freshness and special fragrance. Moreover, the loss of innocence results in the loss of a certain dignity. And this lost innocence is never completely recovered.

In any case, although one does not recover lost innocence, the penitent sinner, according to the doctrine of St. Thomas, finds a bigger treasure. According to St. Gregory, the ravages caused by past transgressions, when seriously pondered, are compensated for by subsequent advantages. They also become the cause for great joy in Heaven. It is like a soldier who takes to his heels and flees the battlefield, but later returns to it. Such a soldier is dearer to his captain than a soldier who remains at his post but is not outstanding for any special act of bravery.[232]

For his part, the merciful Savior grants such favors to the guilty who return to him. He covers them with an effusion of his precious Blood. He knows the situation well, for *where sin increased, grace abounded all the more* (Rom 5: 20). In the words of our Saint, he transforms "our miseries into grace, and thorns into an antidote that leads to our salvation. Remember Job, the very image of a penitent sinner. He received twice what he used to have." [233]

Pious tears

It is here that we witness the triumph of love. An author we have often quoted wonders whether there is a secret to recover lost time. Isn't this as impossible as wanting to bind up a tempest? He replies: "Thank God the secret does exist! Love has invented it. Love has revealed it, so that the love within you can take hold of it. This secret is found in pious tears, though they are not of the eyes. God does not give them to everyone, nor does he ask anyone for them. They are the tears of your heart, of repentance, of the anguish of the soul, and of contrition. With these invisible tears, cover every aspect of your life that has remained sterile. Washed by these tears, those areas will witness the re-entry of love. And who knows! These misspent years may become in God's sight more wonderful, flourishing, and precious because of repentance than they would have been with innocence alone. If you weep like Mary Magdalen, then no one will accuse you of having sinned." [234]

Mary Magdalen's example confirms this doctrine to such an extent that St. Francis de Sales is able to make excellent use of it. It is the crowning glory of all the venerable Doctor's teachings and summarizes this chapter.

Mary Magdalen has a lesson for us

"Mary Magdalen underwent a wonderful conversion. From the soiled and stained creature that she was, she became a pure and clean vessel ready to receive the precious *liquor* of grace. With this she would later anoint her Savior. She was one who, because of her sins, was a foul-smelling heap of manure. After her conversion she became a beautiful lily, a wonderfully perfumed flower. The more she withered and became rancid because of sin, the more she was now purified and renewed by grace.

"We see flowers grow and bloom even from a rotten and smelling mound of earth. We notice that the more the earth is filled with manure and rotten matter, the better the growth and beauty of the flowers planted there.

"In the same way, though completely contaminated by sin, Mary Magdalen, after her conversion, became more beautiful through contrition and love. We can justly call her the advocate of all Christians and all children of the Church. These can be divided into three groups. The first consists of all the just people; the second, of repentant sinners who do not desire to die in sin; and the third, of obstinate and unrepentant sinners who do not care to repent and who die in a state of sin. It is not about this last category that I want to talk, for they have no desire to go to Heaven. Hell is ready for them, and it is their heritage. Their misfortune is proportionate to their obstinacy to die in sin. They are, therefore, damned.

"It is not as one of these sinners that Mary Magdalen is an example, but of those who want to abandon their sinful lives. She was a sinful woman, as the Scriptures teach us: *Mulier erat in civitate peccatrix—a woman of the city, who was a sinner* (Lk 7: 37). She abandoned her sinful life and asked for God's forgiveness with true contrition and a firm resolution to give up sin. In this way, she inspires all sinners to follow her example.

"And as for her repentance, dear God! How large and generous it was! How much she wept for her sins! What did she not do to erase them, both during the lifetime of her Savior and even after his death! She had offended God with all her heart, with all her soul, and with all her body, without reservation. But now she expended herself generously and totally in acts of repentance; she can very rightly be called the patron of all repentant sinners as she surpassed them all through penance.

"We commonly see that if men have been hurt, they want satisfaction in proportion to the wrong done to them. If they have been robbed of a coin, they have to be compensated by another. If a man is harmed by another, it is befitting that he be given compensation in proportion to the harm inflicted on him. In the Old Law it was a case of *'an eye for an eye and a tooth for a tooth.'*

"Well, this law is now abolished among men; nevertheless, in a sense, it is still in force with Jesus Christ and those devoted to his service. For one has to render him as much as one can, in proportion to the fault committed. That is to say, he desires that we do at least as much for him as we have done for the world. This is not asking too much of us. For, if carried away by vain attractions we have done so much for the world, what should we not do for the greater attractions of his grace—which is good and generous. It is not wrong for him to expect this much from us. For just as we used our heart, our soul, our affections, our eyes, our speech, our hair, and our perfume for the world, so also we should use and sacrifice them in the service of Sacred Love."

Advocate of the just

"Mary Magdalen is also the advocate of the just. Even if she is not called virgin, she deserves the name because of the excellence and purity of her self after her conversion. She should be called arch-virgin, more so as she was purified to such an extent in the furnace of Sacred Love that her chastity was reestablished. She was further endowed with such perfect love that, after the Holy

Virgin, she was the one who loved our Lord the most. We can even say that she loved him as much as or more than the seraphs. For it is true that they possess perfect and painless love without fear of losing it. But this saint acquired it after a great deal of work and care, and preserved it with fear and solicitude. In recognition of her fidelity, God gave her a strong and ardent love accompanied by such purity, that just as the Divine Spouse 'wounded' her heart continuously with love, so she 'assaulted' him by sighs, desires, and claims of love. It is believed that she often repeated those words uttered by the spouse in the Song of Songs: *O that you would kiss me with the kisses of your mouth* (Song 1:2). Such a kiss has been greatly desired by human nature and longed for by the Fathers and prophets. This was nothing other than the incarnation and union of the divine with human nature. It was that union with God which this holy lover longed for.

"You see, then, how she is the patron saint of the just. For what could make her more just than this sacred love accompanied by humility and compunction? It entitled her to remain always at the feet of the Savior. He loved her with the same tender and sensitive love that he has for the just." [235]

Architect of mercy

On another occasion, St. Francis de Sales beautifully refers to this illustrious penitent and confirms what we said: "Our Lord restored Mary Magdalen's virginity, not in its original state but after being healed. And this is sometimes of a higher order than that which, though never stained, has perhaps less humility." [236]

Finally, our dear Saint concludes: "Never would the Magdalen have loved her Savior so much if she had not been forgiven so many sins. Never would he have forgiven her so much if she had not committed them. You see, my dear daughter, this great architect of mercy converts our miseries into grace, and transforms the venom of our sins into a salutary medicine for our souls." [237]

11

Devotion to Our Lady

A chapter for our Lady

In preparing the third edition of this book, an idea came to mind: Why not add another chapter? In fact, I considered this an omission, feeling a guilt for not having set it right earlier. For, how can one sing God's mercies without including a single hymn to the Mother of Mercy? To study *the art of profiting from our faults* at the school of St. Francis de Sales, the most loveable of saints, and yet forget the Refuge of Sinners! This does not seem possible. It is true that in the course of this work we touched upon the subject; but it was not enough, for the subject deserves to be treated on its own.

This idea came home to me with greater force at the feet of Our Lady of the Port, at Clermont Ferrand. It is here, at this ancient shrine, that I understood clearly that, for the shipwrecked, Mary is a haven, as well as a guiding star.

St. Francis de Sales was correct in saying: "The Virgin Mary has always remained the polar star and welcome haven of all men sailing the ocean waves of this miserable world. Those who set their course by this divine star will steer clear of the reefs of sin." [238] But even those who have strayed from her protective care will not find a safer haven than the Immaculate Heart of the most tender of mothers. Here they can repair the harm done, as well as *turn it to their advantage*.

It also seems that our good Saint is calling for this

additional chapter. He wants it to harmonize with the preceding pages, where Mary Magdalen was shown to be a model for sinners, keen to correct their mistakes and to turn them to advantage.

Our Lady at the house of Simon the leper

He returns again to the same subject in a letter to St. Jeanne de Chantal. Referring to his prayer during which he is transported to the house in Bethany of Simon the leper, he says: "I saw our Savior, who seemed to me to be in a good mood. However, out of respect for our dear Magdalen, we did not dare approach his feet. We approached his Mother's, who, if I'm not mistaken, was there. I felt ashamed not to have as many tears or such perfume as this saintly penitent. Our Lady, however, was satisfied with a few droplets on the hem of her dress, as we did not dare touch her sacred feet. What followed consoled me a great deal. After dinner, our Lord entrusted his beloved convert to our Lady. We see that from that moment, Mary Magdalen has always been by our Lady's side; and the Blessed Virgin continued to comfort this sinful woman. This gave me courage and infinite joy."[239]

O Blessed Father! Communicate this courage and joyful confidence to all sinners. Let it inspire them to run to Mary. It is possible that, despite all the reasons given in this book, the awareness of their exceeding misery prevents them from throwing themselves completely into the good Heart of Jesus. But, even in this extreme situation, they should throw themselves into the arms of his Mother, whose love for the weakest is guaranteed.

The new Esther

Indeed, our kind Savior wanted it this way. He had foreseen the fears that would arise in us because of his dignity and position as judge, and despite all his goodness. That is why, without ceasing to be our advocate and mediator before God, he condescended to establish between himself and ourselves a mediator and advocate whom we could fearlessly approach. For, as our Mother, she can obtain everything from God. But also, as *his* Mother, she pleads successfully with her Son bcause she was the Mother who had nourished him. Her power of intercession with him is as great as his pleading with his Father, to whom he shows his heart and wounds.

The Fathers of the Church are unanimous in confirming that this truth is in the economy of God's divine plan. According to them, because Jesus is the source of whatever we need, he alone is sufficient to redeem the human race. And yet it was not good for man to be alone. Just as both the sexes were involved in our downfall, so also both should contribute to its redemption.[240] That is why the Redeemer left the ransom of the human race in Mary's hands.[241] He wanted everything to come through her mediation.[242] She is the viaduct through which water flows to us, the ladder leading us to God, the door opening onto his goodness, the means by which all the merits of the Divine Head come to the body of the Church. No one can be saved, no one can be forgiven, except through her.[243]

As the new Esther, she has been found acceptable in the Lord's sight, for all men in his empire have been given to her. She holds the scepter of mercy, while her Son remains the King of justice.[244]

Yes, Mary is the minister plenipotentiary of mercy. Mercy is her department. In our present political system, if someone has a problem regarding the ministry of finance, fishing, or agriculture, he addresses the minister in charge of the respective portfolio. Mary is to be approached by those in need of mercy. And the more serious their misery, the greater right they have to her maternal love.

Deep calls to deep (Ps 42:7), or, as St. Francis de Sales expressed it: "Nothing can be more welcome to generous abundance than needy poverty. And the greater the abundance of goodness, the stronger the inclination to distribute and share it with others. Indeed, it would be difficult to judge who possesses joy in greater measure: generous abundance seeking to spread and communicate itself, or poverty . . . failing and in need of receiving. Our Lord makes our choice easier when he says, *It is better to give than to receive!* [245]

Mary as Mediatrix

St. Anselm goes further. He has no hesitation in saying that very often one's prayers are more speedily answered if one invokes the name of Mary than by invoking the name of Jesus. "It is not," he adds "that the Mother is more powerful than the Son, since it is from him that she derives her power. But Jesus, being the judge and master of all men, discerns each one's merits and confines himself to justice before answering. Whereas in the name of Mary, his satisfying justice is all appeased, and the merits of this incomparable creature intervene and obtain everything." [246]

Ancient writers, supported by Sacred Scripture, reveal to us this enchanting mystery in their commentaries. In the Old Testament, they say, God is given names: Lord of the Armies, God of Vengeance, Lion of the tribe of Judah. He is represented as surrounded by fire, thundering from the heavens, hurling thunder, sharpening the sword, bending bows, shooting off arrows. We see him bury the earth under flood waters, destroy guilty cities under sulphur rain, drown his enemies in swirling sea waters, or we see him burying them in the earth that his anger has partly opened up. All of a sudden, the same God appears in the Gospels and takes on the appearance of a Lamb. He does not seem to have the courage to squash a half-broken reed, or to extinguish the still-smoking wick. What has happened? God has taken on flesh in the womb of Mary.

The sun while passing through the Zodiac signs of Gemini, Cancer, and Leo pours down torrid heat. These rays soften and become salutary as soon as the sun enters Virgo,[247] just as the unicorn, when it lays its head in the lap of a young girl, forgets its savage ferocity and becomes tame. So too, the Sun of Justice becomes a benign star, changing his heart of anger to a gentle warmth as soon as he hides his splendid radiance within the womb of the Virgin of Nazareth. Justice stays on in the Heavens, and mercy descends to inhabit the earth. No more anger, no more indignation after the virgin earth of Mary's womb has borne its fruit.[248]

Within the womb of the gentlest of women, the Lion of Judah has taken on the soft wool and the natural weakness of the lamb. From the milk of his Mother, he has drawn out the gentleness of this tender sheep. *Milk is better than wine,* says an illustrious interpreter of the Song of Songs. Wine can intoxicate a man, make him forget the injuries he has received, and make it easier for him to forgive. The milk of the Blessed Virgin has the power to intoxicate God. He has hardly begun to drink when he imbibes mercy and removes the memory of our sins, so as to forgive us generously.[249] Richard of St. Victor is not afraid to add: "Yes. It is in you, O Mary, that we find the accumulated abundance of God's mercy, and it is from there that it has flowed on to us."[250] Honey has come out from the rock because from the branch of Jesse has blossomed the flower that provides this sweet juice, the cure for all our evils.[251]

Appealing to the Bride

While crossing the Red Sea, the Egyptians, who symbolize sinners, were swallowed up by angry waves. There was no Ark there. However, when the Jordan was crossed there were no victims. The Ark of the Covenant, the Seat of Mercy, kept all chastisement at a distance. Without Mary, there is every reason to fear God's vengeance. But with God dwelling in the propitiatory ark, one expects nothing but blessings. So also, as long as Simon sees the Messiah in the arms of his Mother, he proclaims Israel's salvation. And when he holds him in his own arms, he sees in him the destruction and the resurrection of many.[252] O sinner! you should tremble if you separate Christ from Mary. But when you are in the arms of this loving Queen, pray to him full of trust. For she is mercy on his pedestal, the flower on his branch, the water in his ocean.

The Son of God, made Man, while in the bosom of the Father, drew out the attributes of divine fatherhood. He clothed himself with motherly feelings while in the bosom of his Mother. Taking an authoritative text of St. Ambrose, a famous theologian[253] concludes effortlessly: Mary increased the clemency of the God she begot and crowned his head with a diadem of eternal mercy.

The same theologian adds: Truly foolish were the virgins who slept without oil in their lamps. But still more foolish were they when, after being spurned by the bridegroom, they did not beseech the help of the bride, that is to say, Mary. They cry out, *Lord, Lord, open to us.*[254] They appeal to the Judge. From his justice they get the answer they deserved. *I do not know you*. Why did they not appeal to the Bride and cry out: "Our Lady! Our Lady!" With this name alone, they would have received their favor.

Invoking Mary's name

O sinner! whoever you are, and even if one foot is already in Hell, and your heart is full of despair, look at Mary. Think of her,[255] and you will regain your innocence and peace. It is the Virgin Mary herself who revealed to St. Brigid that anyone (unless he has been already damned) who invokes her name will get rid of his sins. The devil, for his part, will take to his heels no sooner than he hears the name of Mary being invoked.[256] The Apostle of Chablais narrates the following incident: A frightened bird was caught by a sparrow-hawk. However, the sparrow-hawk, on hearing the name of Mary uttered by the bird, released its prey. This bird had learned that name in the monastery. If such be the case of a bird, then will the sinner not escape from the claws of Satan if he invokes this all-powerful name? According to the sacred text, her name should be *spiraculum hominis*, our breath. In fact, a Father of the Church says it is through Mary that the guilty soul breathes and prepares to obtain forgiveness.

A modern writer is still more explicit. In a daring comparison, he points out the role of the Mother of God for those whom sin has wounded or killed. "Every heartbeat has a double action and is made up of two movements. While one draws in the used blood from the organs, the other releases fresh blood. This is because the heart itself is double. It is as if two hearts are in one: one more active and the other more passive; one that gives life, the other that takes death back and replaces it with life. One verifies, while the other purifies.

In the midst of a regenerated world, such is also the role of the Heart, of this Heart made up of two souls living in one, the soul of Jesus and the soul of Mary. The soul of Jesus is the living side of the world's heart. The soul of Mary is, by the grace of Jesus, the side through which what is dead returns to life.

It carries humanity's dead blood to him who is Life itself. And from there, once renewed, it is sent back by Jesus into the world, alive and divine. The Word, through the Incarnation, has deified the blood. But it is the Virgin who gave the Word the matter to be deified."[257]

Big sinners repent

Who would ever be able to count the number of souls that the Mother of God has brought back to divine life! For this, one would need to list *all* the conversions. Not a single conversion could take place without her motherly help. According to St. Ignatius the Martyr, it is impossible for a sinner to be saved without the help of Mary. One is not saved by the justice of God, but rather by his infinite mercy, and that is solicited by Mary's prayers.[258]

St. Bonaventure adds that, like the new Ruth, Mary gleans the ears of corn that have escaped the harvesters' attention. He is referring to those souls who remain deaf to all other appeals of grace. She brings them together and places them back again in the granary of the Father of the family.

According to St. Peter Damian, it is through the prayers of the Blessed Virgin that the thief on Calvary repented and became a martyr. Judas, the traitor, would never have been lost had he only delayed his suicide until after the dying Christ had entrusted his followers to his Mother.[259]

It is to her that the Prince of Apostles has recourse after his triple denial. In poetic language, St. Gregory of Nazianzen shows her pleading with her Son: "O Word of God, it is man's nature to sin; forgive Peter." And Jesus replies: "You know, Mother mine, that I comply with all your wishes. Out of consideration for you, I forgive Peter all his mistakes." St. Paul, according to some ancient biographers,[260] attributed the sudden grace of his conversion to the intercession of the Mother of God.

Mary's glory in Heaven

According to St. Bonaventure, if such was the mercy shown by Mary during her exile on earth, how much greater will it be now that she reigns in Heaven?[261] Her mercy increases in proportion to the crowds of miserable persons whom she sees on earth. For the Church herself says that her work in Paradise is to pray for sinners.[262] Isn't it because of them that she owes an infinite increase in her glory? Would she be the Mother of the Redeemer if there had not been sinners to redeem? "This truth has been excellently summed up by Mr. Olier when he says: 'It is due to sinners that the blessed Virgin obtained the happiness of being the mother of the Savior of men.' For if there were no sin, Jesus would not have come into this world in the garb of sinful flesh."[263] In that sense, then, Mary owes her status of Mother of Jesus Christ to sinners.

"According to St. Thomas of Villanova,[264] it is we who in some way have provided the occasion for her promotion. Unless there was on earth the sickness of sin to cure, the Divine Doctor would never have descended. It is because of our sinful condition that Mary became the Mother of God. God would never have become man if man had never sinned.[265] O Virgin! Without doubt, you owe us nothing, since it is our demerit and not your merit that has brought about this state of affairs. You are truly the advocate of sinners: because of their sins, you have been elevated to such a high position. Our sins fill us with a sincere repentance, and we feel proud of your sublimity, and your glory compensates for the damage caused by our faults."

Renewal of divine sonship

A spiritual writer exclaims: How could I despair, O Mary, despite the enormity of my crimes! For you, Mary, are the mother of all men but especially of sinners![266]

Yes, it is sinners who obtain the incessant re-creation of the glories and joys of divine motherhood for this august Virgin. For as often as she brings Christ to live again within them, she is in fact giving birth to Christ.[267]

Every sinner's conversion is a rebirth to grace. Every renewal of divine sonship comes with being reunited with the Savior, and living in Christ[268] again. The sinner then gives the heavenly Father an occasion to say: *You are my son, today I have begotten you.*[269] The guardian angel of the happy convert, showing him to Mary, salutes her in the words of Elizabeth: *Blessed are you among women*, for truly, he is the fruit of her womb.

Mary is the mother of the members as well as of the Head of the mystical body of the Church. Not one just soul can be formed without having been engendered by the new Eve, by the real Mother of all the living beings.

From goats to lambs

While commenting on the text *Pasce hedos meos* (feed my goats), an ancient interpreter of the Song of Songs [270] has no difficulty in applying it to Mary with regard to sinners. They, indeed, are the he-goats, he says; and very correctly they are called the goats of Mary. No, certainly not because she would like them as they are in their present condition, to be placed on the left side of the Judge. They are goats of Mary because she adopts them in order to ensure for them a place on his right by transforming them into faithful sheep. That is why, in common parlance, a doctor addresses a patient as *his* patient, the one whose cure he desires, not the sickness.

Of course, a lamb is preferable to a goat. So also, nothing is worth the straightforwardness of an innocent soul. Happy are they who like spotless lambs are worthy of being fondled by the Virgin of Virgins, aptly called the Divine Shepherdess. This truth remains a great consolation for sinners. They admit that their crimes have merited for them a place like the accursed goats, to the left of the Judge. And yet it depends on them alone to approach Mary with confidence, and become *her goats*, soon to be changed into lambs.

Health, similarly, will always be preferable to sickness. He, indeed, is lucky who doesn't require a doctor. But once sick, what assurance and joy it is to be under the treatment of a prince of medical science, to be his client and to be numbered among *his patients*.

However weak we are, however desperate the state of our soul, Mary will adopt us as *her patients* if we wish it. And inasmuch as no spiritual infirmity here on earth is incurable, because none can resist the treatment of the All-powerful Mother of God, she will heal us. Her glory, like that of an expert doctor, will shine in proportion to the seriousness of the evil she has to cure. Her fame, similar to that of an expert doctor, will shine in proportion to the gravity of the sickness she has to heal.

Then, after being healed and snatched from death, this loving Mother will love us and watch over us all through the weakness and dangers of a life-long convalescence, like a doctor who checks on his patients after their cure. We will now have a special right to her motherly protection. It will be an honor for her to be interested in our persevering in the state of grace that she has acquired for us at the price of her prayers and sufferings.

Shall we remain unfaithful to her and fall again into sin? Does the doctor desert and let his patients relapse? Is he going to take revenge on us for not being docile enough to take his prescriptions? Will he not, rather, redouble his efforts to tax his talent and dedication to effect a more difficult cure?

Conclusion

O most good Mother of him who said: *It is not the healthy who need a doctor*, and again, *Forgive seventy times seven*. Will they exhaust your power in the tenderness of your care? According to your St. Bonaventure,[271] your devoted saint, you will go to seek the sinner rejected by all. You will embrace and warm him. You will not rest till you have cured him.

Tuus sum ego, salvum me fac: I am your patient, save me.[272] Such will be my cry of hope all the days of my exile. The more I recall my past falls, the more I will remind you that you have the power and goodness to lift me up. And the more will I rest assured that you have not abandoned me and left me half-cured.

My gratitude for your care and the desire to manifest your power will help me to follow your counsels. I will love you, *I will glorify you* because you *have delivered my soul from the depths of Sheol*.[273] And finally, in Heaven, I will modestly take my seat among these who owe their salvation to you because in their misery they trusted in you. I will remain your pride—just as the patient is the pride of the doctor who has snatched him from the portals of death, not only once but several times. This will be the greatest gain that grace has gained. My very mistakes will become a pedestal to your glory, while at the throne of God's mercies I will sing forever: *Misericordias Domini in aeternum cantabo*—I will sing of thy steadfast love, O LORD, forever.[274]

Amen! Amen! Amen!

Notes

CHAPTER 1

1. Sermon for the First Sunday of Lent.
2. Talk 16, On Distasteful Things.
3. Letter 333 (Blaise collection).
4. Talk 20, On Religious Aspirations.
5. Letter 428.
6. Letter to a young lady 847.
7. Letter to a lady.
8. Letter 847.
9. Sermon for the First Sunday of Lent.
10. *Introduction to the Devout Life.*
11. Letter 795.
12. Letter to a lady.
13. Talk 3, On Firmness.
14. Talk 9, On Modesty.
15. Letter to St. Jeanne Francoise de Chantal 332.
16. Talk 9, On Modesty.
17. *Manual for the Direction of Saints.*
18. *Ad Theod. laps.*, book 1, no. 1.
19. *Treatise on the Love of God.*
20. Letter 740.
21. Letter 53.
22. Letter to his sister, wife of Cormillian, 761.
23. *Introduction to the Devout Life.*

CHAPTER 2

24. *Introduction to the Devout Life*, 4, 12.
25. 1 Kings 19:2.
26. *Introduction to the Devout Life*, 4, 12.
27. Letter 173.
28. Gal 5:7.
29. Fr. La Rivière, *Life of Blessed Francis de Sales.*
30. *Introduction to the Devout Life*, 1, 5.
31. Letter to St. Jeanne de Chantal 59.
32. *Spiritual Works.*
33. Talk 10, On Obedience.
34. *Treatise on the Love of God*, 9, 7.
35. *Treatise on the Love of God*, 10, 7.
36. Letter to a lady from Cornillon.
37. Letter to a Mother Superior of the Visitation 756.
38. Letter to a lady 185.
39. Letter to a young lady 2.
40. Letter to lady President Brulart 90.
41. Letter to the Abbess of Puits-d'Orbe 53.
42. Letter to a nun 732.
43. Letter to a young lady 480.
44. Letter to a lady 833.
45. Letter 186.
46. Sister Fichet, M.A., *Holy Year of the Visitation*, 11, 5.
47. Mother de la Roche, C. A. Joly, *Spiritual Advice.*
48. *Vie escrité par elle-même*, 30.
49. Fr. J. J. Allemand.

50. Talk 14, On the Particular Judgment.
51. *Introduction to the Devout Life*, 3, 9.
52. Talk 2, On Confidence.
53. Talk 14, On the Particular Judgment.
54. Talk 3, On Firmness.
55. Letter to the Abbess of Puits-d'Orbe 53.
56. Mother de la Roche, C. A. Joly, *Spiritual Advice.*
57. Letter to a nun 261.
58. Letter to a lady 800.
59. Letter to a lady 151.
60. *Introduction to the Devout Life*, 3, 9.
61. Fr. La Rivière, *Life of Blessed Francis de Sales*, 3, 9.

CHAPTER 3

62. Homily, *De Poenit.*
63. *Ad Theod. laps.*, 1.
64. Letters 35 and 5.
65. *De sermone Domini in monte*, book 1.
66. *The Progress of the Soul.*
67. Letter to a lady 771.
68. Letter to a young lady 837.
69. Letter to a lady 820.
70. Letter to the Abbess of Puits-d'Orbe 235.
71. Letter to a lady 833.
72. Talk 14, On the Particular Judgment.
73. Talk 20, On Religious Aspirations: *Non est grave certamen cadere, sed in lapsu manere* (St. John Chrysostom, *Ad Theod. laps.*, 1).
74. Letter to a Superior of the Visitation 706.
75. Letter to a sister 761.
76. Letter to a nun 784.
77. Letter to the lady President of Herce 212.
78. *Introduction to the Devout Life*, 4, 2.
79. Letter to St. Jeanne de Chantal 332.
80. Sermon for the First Sunday of Lent.
81. *Introduction to the Devout Life*, 1, 5.
82. Letter to a lady 814.
83. Letter to a lady 831.
84. Letter to a lady 839.
85. Letter to a lady 173.
86. Letter to a nun 717.
87. Sermon for the Fourth Sunday of Advent.
88. Sister E. C. of Tours, sacristan of the first convent of the Visitation of Annecy. Declaration on the miracles and favors worked at the tomb of Blessed Francis de Sales.

CHAPTER 4

89. *Epist. 82 ad Oger.*
90. *Hoc opus nostrae salutis/ Ordo depoposcerat,/ Multiformis proditoris/ Ars ut artem falleret,/ Et medelam feret inde/ Hostis unde laeserat* (Hymm of the Passion).
91. *Homily to the people of Antioch.*
92. *De corrupt. et grat.*, I; see also St. Thomas's commentary on this text of St. Paul.
93. Letter 813.
94. Letter to a lady 641.
95. Letter 173.

96. Sermon for the Third Sunday of Advent.
97. St. John Chrysostom.
98. Sir 10:13.
99. St. Thomas Aquinas, *Catena aurea, in 2 ad Cor.*
100. Sermon for the Feast of the Purification.
101. *Introduction to the Devout Life*, 3, 6.
102. Letter to a lady 883.
103. Talk 3, On Firmness.
104. Letter to a young lady 811.
105. Letter to a Carmelite Superior 740.
106. Letter to a Superior 449.
107. See Ps 58:1.
108. Dan 5:27.
109. See Hag 1:9.
110. Jer 3:1.
111. Segneri, *Manna dell' anima*, 20 June.
112. Letter to a nun 741.
113. Letter to a lady, 8 April 1602.
114. Letter to a lady 825.
115. Letter to a Bernardine nun 870.
116. Letter to a lady 313.
117. Letter to a young lady 811.
118. See *Catena Aurea*, 2 Cor, 2a–2ae, q. 162 ad 6.
119. Exhortation 1, *Ad Stagyr.*, 9.
120. *De compunctione*, book 3, 9.
121. Homily on the Publican and the Pharisee.
122. *Contra Donat.*, book 2.
123. Sermon 1, *super Missus.*
124. Sister C.-E. Cortelot, *Holy Year of the Visitation*, 14 November.
125. Jas 4:6.
126. Practiced by Fr. J. J. Allemand.
127. Letter to Bishop Rey of Annecy.
128. Sir 11:25.
129. *The heart of St. Gertrude*, by R. P. Gros, S.J.
130. Sermon for the First Sunday in Lent.
131. *Introduction to the Devout Life*, 1, 12.
132. *Introduction to the Devout Life*, 3, 5.
133. Homily for All Saints' Day.
134. *Introduction to the Devout Life*, 1, 12.
135. Letter to the Abbess of Puits-d'Orbe.
136. Homily on Peter and Elias.
137. *De gradibus humilit.*, 3.
138. Book 1, ch. 2.

CHAPTER 5

139. *Introduction to the Devout Life*, 3, 6.
140. Talk 10, On Obedience.
141. Talk 18, On the Sacraments.
142. Mr. de Bernières, *Chrétien Intérieur*, I, III, 16.
143. Mother Mary de Sales Chappuis.
144. Ps 4:2.
145. Sister M. A. de Mayen, *Holy Year of the Visitation*, 16 March.
146. Letter to St. Jeanne de Chantal 130.
147. Talk 4, On Cordiality.
148. Holy Year of the Visitation, 3 March.
149. Letter to a lady 808.
150. *The Imitation of Christ*, book III, ch. 46,.
151. Mr. de Bernières, *Chrétien Intérieur*.

152. *Introduction to the Devout Life*, 3, 6.
153. Letter to St. Jeanne de Chantal 100.
154. *Introduction to the Devout Life*, 3, 6.
155. Talk 4, On Cordiality.
156. Talk 16, On Aversions.
157. *On Mother M. Melanie Pommeroy*, Circular of the Visitation of Thonon (1872).
158. Letter to a religious 715.
159. Talk 11, On Obedience.
160. *In Cant. Sermo X*, 5.
161. P. Gaud, *Treatise on Christian Hope*.
162. *Holy Year of the Visitation*, 11 January, Life of Sister F. G. de la Grave.

CHAPTER 6

163. *On Life and Christian Virtues*: On Hope.
164. Homily by Msgr. Pie, All Saints' Day, 1 November 1871.
165. Ven. Alexander of St. Francis, a Carmelite who died in 1630, *Manuale pauperum*, ch. 38.
166. *Cristiano instruito*, II, 7, 16.
167. First Sermon on the Nativity of the Blessed Virgin.
168. Sermon for Good Friday.
169. St. Bernard says the same thing: "The Father of Mercy is necessarily the Father of the miserable."
170. Ven. Alexander of St. Francis, *Manuale pauperum*, ch. 38.
171. Letter of Fr. Varin, 2 September 1805.
172. St. Epiphanius, *Physiologist*.
173. *Complete Works*, II, 473ff.
174. Letter 89.

CHAPTER 7

175. Talk 2, On Confidence.
176. Letter to a Mother Superior of the Visitation 428.
177. Letter to St. Jeanne de Chantal 84.
178. Letter to a lady. The Church does not have any other doctrine. In her liturgical prayers she exhorts us to present to God, to the Virgin Mary, and to the saints our position as sinners as the most appropriate one for receiving their protection.
179. Letter to a lady at Aix 889.
180. Letter to a young lady 829.
181. *Complete Works*, XIV, 236.
182. Letter to a lady 838.
183. Letter to a lady 406.
184. Sermon for the Feast of St. John, *ante Portam Latinam*.
185. Letter to Mother Angela Arnauld, Abbess of Port Royal.
186. *Complete Works*, XIX, 196.
187. *Advice to Confessors*, 2, 196.
188. *Spirit of St. Francis de Sales*, III, ch. 14, s. 28.
189. Fr. La Rivière, *Life of the Blessed Francis de Sales*, 3, 9.

CHAPTER 8

190. Homily 7, On Penance.
191. Homily 4, On Penance.
192. Victor, *Episc. Cart.*
193. Letter, 22 March 1614.
194. Letter to a young lady 811.
195. Talk 17, On Aversions.

196. *The Director for Christian Perfection*, 20.
197. *Ad Theod. laps.*, book 2, 1.
198. *Physiologist*, ch. 5, *De cervo*.
199. Fr. Grou, *Manual for Interior Souls*.
200. Letter to a lady 835.
201. Letter to nun 734.
202. Letter 764.
203. Letter to a lady 275.
204. Letter to a lady 802.
205. Letter 764.
206. Letter to his niece 308.
207. Letter to a noble 836.
208. Letter to a lady 882.
209. Letter to a lady 186.
210. Letter to a novice 45.
211. *Treatise on the Love of God*, 11, 17.

CHAPTER 9

212. Letter to a lady 787.
213. *Introduction to the Devout Life*, 1, 19.
214. *Introduction to the Devout Life*, 2, 19.
215. *Advice to Confessors*.
216. Letter to a Mother Favre 361.
217. *Treatise on the Love of God*, 2, 20. Here the author plays on the French word *ardent*, which means the water of life (*eau-de vie*) and "burning water."
218. *Treatise on the Love of God*, 2, 20.
219. Ibid., 11, 12.
220. St. Bernard, *Canticle of Canticles*, serm. 10.
221. Religious exchange on the Visitation of Turin, death in the fragrance of holiness, on 5 December 1692.
222. Hos 13:14; 1 Cor 15:54.

CHAPTER 10

223. *Treatise on the Love of God*, 1, 11, 21.
224. Letter 449.
225. St. Thomas Aquinas, *Summa Theologia*, suppl. 12, a. 3.
226. Letter to a lady 585.
227. *Treatise on the Love of God*, 1, 4, 6.
228. Sermon for the Feast of the Presentation.
229. Instruction 12.
230. *De apologia David*, ch. 2.
231. *Ad Theod. laps.*, I, ch. 2.
232. St. Thomas Aquinas, *Summa Theologia*, IIIa, q. 89, a. 3.
233. *Treatise on the Love of God*, 1, 11, 12ff.
234. Msgr. C. Gay, *On Life and Christian Virtues*: On Charity.
235. Sermon for the Feast of St. Mary Magdalen.
236. Talk 19, On the Virtues of St. Joseph.
237. Letter 392.

CHAPTER 11

238. Sermon for Christmas Eve.
239. Sermon for the Annunciation.
240. St. Bernard, Sermon of the Assumption.
241. St. Bernard, Sermon 2, On the Nativity.
242. Ibid.
243. St. Germain of Constantinople, *Orat. de Zona*.
244. St. Thomas Aquinas, *In Esther*.
245. *Treatise on the Love of God*, 1, 15.

246. *De excell. Virg.*, c. 6.
247. St. Anthony, 4, 15, 21.
248. See Psalm 84.
249. Card. Hailgrin.
250. *In Cantic.* 2, 23.
251. Hugo de St-Victor, *Miscell.*, 2, 4, 26.
252. Lk 2:34.
253. Christophe de Vega, *Theologia mariana.*
254. Mt 25:11.
255. St. Bernard, Homily 2 on the Nativity.
256. *Revelat.*, 1, 9.
257. P. Gratry, *Month of Mary of the Immaculate Conception.*
258. *Apud Celada, de Judith figurata,* c. 10, no. 69.
259. Philippe Abbas.
260. See *Cornel. a Lap. in act.*, 7.
261. *Spec.*, ch. 8.
262. Secret for the Vigil of the Assumption.
263. *Interior Life of the Very Saintly Virgin,* 352.
264. Quoted by the annotator of Mr. Olier.
265. Such at least is the theory of the great Thomist school. According to St. Francis de Sales, the Word would have taken flesh even if man had not sinned. But in this hypothesis, Mary would not have the glory due her brought about by her suffering, and for which glory, in a sense, she is indebted to sinners.
266. *Laurent. a Pointe.*
267. Borgius de Gubbio, 9: *De signis Ecclesiae.*
268. Ephesians ch. 2.
269. Psalm 2.
270. *Guillelm. apud Delrio in Cant.*
271. *Spec.*, ch. 5.
272. Psalm 118 (see 119:94).
273. Ps 86:13.
274. Ps 89:1.